This book is dedicated to my sons, Jonah and Ariel. You are the inspiration for this book, and junior modern-day Maccabees. —A. G.

Table of Contents

Acknowledgments

While my name is on the cover of this book, *Modern-Day Maccabees* would never have become a reality without the love and support of many. Thank you goes to all of the athletes who agreed to be a part of this project and embraced it enthusiastically. You continue to inspire me and, thanks to this book, hopefully will inspire many more around the world. I would like to thank all those (in no particular order) who coordinated interviews with the athletes: Liron Fanan, Joe Bick, Sean Kelso, Matt Provence, Mike Herman, Shlomi Pe'er, David Pick, Noam Galai, Ann Laney, and Brooke Scheyer.

Special thanks to Bryan and Max Kanefield for the specially designed Sports Word Puzzles in the book. To order your subscription, check out www.gamedaypublishing.com.

Thanks to dear friends who helped in a myriad of ways, from concept to publication, go to:

Steve Rabinowitz, Laurie Moskowitz, Abbey Frank, Yonah Mishaan, Steve Leibowitz, Amy Martin, Josh Hasten, Bonnie Wilensky, Larry Kenigsberg, Big Mike Gondelman, Neil Amrani, Jasmine Marcus, Jeremy Last, Yossi Goldstein, and all my Kickstarter supporters.

Gavri Yares, for filming and editing. Keep coming on Friday night. My kids and many others, I think, consider you one of their "modern-day Maccabees."

Ari Louis, my broadcast partner for two years and cofounder of Israel Sports Radio, who always makes me laugh and teaches me about boxing and the WNBA. You are truly the greatest cohost anyone could ask for.

Thanks to those who have given me a platform to write: *Washington Jewish Week*, especially Phil Jacobs and Meredith Jacobs, Jewish Telegraphic Agency, The LA *Jewish Journal*, *The Jerusalem Post*, and Uriel Sturm.

Josh Halickman, cofounder of Israel Sports Radio, for your ideas for this project.

Special thanks go to Jim Williams for writing the foreword to this book and for being a dear friend. Thanks for all your help and support for my projects both in Israel and the United States.

To my illustrator, cousin, and friend Jess Norris, thank you so much! Your creative energy is so appreciated. Thanks for putting up with all my last-minute requests and changes.

Family thanks go to: cousins Lisa and Ross Breen, Neal Hecht, David and Hana Hecht, Natalie and Mike Frady, Faye Brown, Linda and Mike Bott, Ellen Norris, Wright Norris, Sharon Silverman and Tina Richards , Joanne Silverman, Steve Silverman, Arthur and Beverly Radin, Stephen and Laura Lasky, Beth Lasky and Richard Hijazi.

Aunts Marcia Silverman, Sheila Hecht, Elaine Brown, and Cynthia Glazer, who put up with watching sports, even when you didn't want to.

Uncles Jerry Hecht, Jerry Brown, and Stuart Silverman, who shared with me their passion for sports and Judaism. Though gone, your impact on my life does not diminish.

My brother, David, and sister, Debra, who, along with their spouses Beth and Jason, have always encouraged and supported my many projects, small and large.

My family on the other side of the pond, Malka and Jay Neustadter: I wrote this book for your kids, in whom you have worked to inspire a love of American sports along with the many other wonderful values. Of all the things I cherished while in Israel for two years, getting to spend time with you and your kids is certainly at the top of my list.

My father-in-law, Dr. Albert Dreisinger, thank you for your continued support.

My father, Sigmund Gershman. You will never know how much you are missed. Your humor, inspiration, and entrepreneurial spirit certainly lives on. I will never forget the last game we went to together.

My mother, Cissy Gershman. You always said you taught my father everything he knew about sports. You have been the number one modern-day Maccabee in my life, and I thank you for the unconditional love, support, and inspiration you offer continuously in all things, especially sports and Judaism.

My wife, Aviva. Thanks for being my personal editor, partner, and best friend. The saying goes "The greatest thing a man can do for his kids is love their mother," and I certainly can say every day that I love you!

Foreword

For some of us, sports are a very important part of our lives.

If we are fortunate enough, we can play sports competitively. Maybe we will play for our team at school, or perhaps in a league where we play after school and during the summer. Be it Little League or soccer, competitive sports can be a great deal of fun and enrich our lives in many ways.

But we don't have to play sports in a league. We can enjoy just being part of a pickup game in our neighborhood, or watch our favorite team on television, and sports still can have an impact on our lives.

It does not matter at what level we participate. It is how we use sports to enrich our life that is the most important thing.

As Jews we are taught that understanding and obeying the rules are a very important part of our everyday lives. Every sport that we play comes with its own unique set of rules, and thus we learn the single most important accomplishment in sports is that of sportsmanship. Playing by the rules and understanding the importance of the proper way to win with humility and to lose knowing that you gave your best effort is, in its own way, a major accomplishment.

Judaism teaches us that we must respect and learn from those who teach us, and therefore, paying attention to coaches, managers, and mentors is very important. Kevin Youkilis, the star third baseman of the Boston Red Sox, (at the time of publication) is a three-time All-Star and a two-time World Series winner. As a young Jewish boy growing up in Cincinnati, Ohio, his great talent would have never been realized had he not followed the advice and the teachings of his coaches, starting back in Little League.

As a young Jewish girl growing up in Tampa, Florida, Morgan Pressel used her faith to get her through losing her mother to breast cancer. Morgan was just fifteen when her mother died, yet just two years later, at the age of seventeen, she began her career as a golfer on the LPGA Tour.

As you read this book, you will realize that what makes these athletes so extraordinary is not just their exceptional talents, but it is what they learned as young Jews growing up in their homes and in their communities that made them the role models they are today.

You should be very, very proud of the people who are included in this book because they did things the right way and are worthy of being called stars. But the most important thing to understand is that they learned at an early age to always play by the rules, how to handle winning and losing, and to make sure that what their coaches and managers told them through "teachable moments" was something they never forgot.

Also, each athlete in this book understands the importance of *tzedakah* and giving back to their community. Whether it is through a charitable foundation or fund-raisers, each person in this book understand the great responsibility that comes with success.

While very few of us will ever become professional athletes, we can still love sports. What we learn from sports can be applied to every area of life. To be successful, one must always learn the value of teamwork, the importance that playing by the rules has in everyday life, and most of all, that to be a winner in life, paying attention to our teachers will, in the end, make us all-stars in whatever career we choose. –J. W.

Introduction

The idea for this book can be traced back easily to my days as a kid growing up in Richmond, Virginia. Every week I would eagerly anticipate Thursday afternoon, when the local *Richmond Jewish News* would come to the house. I would fly in the door from school, grab the paper, and flip to the back. It was a thrill for me to see what each Jewish athlete was accomplishing, locally and globally. Their inspiring example gave me the determination to be a proud Jew and an aspiring, yet ethical, athlete.

While my career on the court or field never blossomed to the level of the athletes featured in this book, my pride in things Jewish, including athletes, continues to grow. I hope *Modern-Day Maccabees*, with its twenty-first-century role models, will excite and inspire you to dream big, as a Jew and an athlete.

It is always a tricky thing to make a list of anyone "Jewish." While this is not a book about religion, it includes only Jewish athletes who are defined by Jewish law as Jewish. In addition, all athletes featured in this book were chosen because they proudly claim their Judaism and are currently outstanding in their respective sports. Of the twenty athletes and stories featured in *Modern-Day Maccabees*, fifteen were interviewed by me. Some of the sports stars here even wrote personal letters of advice to *you*, the kids reading this book!

I was picky in choosing the athletes, and not all great players could be included, most notably Ryan Braun and Ian Kinsler. The profiles featured are organized according to the "four major sports" in the United States, baseball, football, basketball, and hockey. Surprise solo athletes are also included, so get reading and find out who they are! Have a great time reading this book, and I hope it inspires you to be proud, work hard, and aim high!

*Author's note: All facts presented in this book were accurate when this book went to press in June 2012.

Baseball

Ike Davis

Did You Know? Ike Davis was drafted in the 2005 amateur draft by the Tampa Bay Devil Rays, but decided to attend Arizona State University instead.

Jewish Pride

In an interview Ike did with the Jewish Channel in 2010, he said, "I'm proud to have Jewish blood in me. I think it's made me better because I'm kind of a diverse guy."

Biography

Isaac "Ike" Davis was born March 22, 1987, in Edina, Minnesota. As the son of Major League Baseball pitcher Ron Davis, Ike grew up playing baseball. He attended his father's baseball camps and was coached by his father at a young age.

Ike starred as a high school baseball player at Chaparral High School in Scottsdale, Arizona. He led his team to three Arizona State Championships, broke records for batting, and was named the Arizona 4A Pitcher of the Year his junior year. As a senior, Ike was named a high school All-American.

Although Ike was drafted in 2005 by the Tampa Bay Devil Rays, he went on to play three years at Arizona State University after high school. During his time at ASU, Ike received numerous honors, such as Pac-10 Conference and All-American honors. Upon the completion of his junior year of college, Ike was selected in the first round of the 2008 amateur draft by the New York Mets.

Ike played for the Mets minor-league teams Brooklyn, St. Lucie, Binghamton, and Buffalo until April 19, 2010, when he made his major-league debut at Citi Field against the Chicago Cubs. He had two hits in his first game with the Mets. Ike ended his rookie season batting .264 with 138 hits and 19 home runs in 147 games. His second season was cut short due to injury, and Ike played in only 36 games. Ike Davis is under contract with the New York Mets until 2017.

Ike Davis's Career Highlights

2003 - Member of the gold medal United States World Youth Championship team
2004 - MVP, AFLAC All-American High School Baseball Classic
2006 - Rivals.com first-team freshman All-American
2007 - Named to the Arizona State University All-Decade Team
2008 - Drafted in the first round by the New York Mets
2010 - April 19, 2010 major-league debut

Mitzvah Moments

In 2009, Ike's friend and baseball teammate from high school, Michael Lio, died from Ewing's sarcoma. Ike has helped to raise money to "strike out children's cancer." He has been a part of charity dinners and fishing trips whose proceeds have been given to Solving Kids' Cancer and the Liddy Shriver Sarcoma Initiative. Ike has also donated proceeds from "I Like Ike" T-shirts to Ewing's sarcoma research.

Team Player

Ike has been a member of two gold medal teams in his baseball career. In 2003, he was a member of the United States World Youth Championship team that won gold in Taiwan. Additionally, Ike won gold when he represented America as a member of Team USA in the 2009 Baseball World Cup in Nettuno, Italy.

All in the Family

Ike's father, Ron Davis, was a major-league relief pitcher for eleven years with the New York Yankees, Minnesota Twins, Chicago Cubs, Los Angeles Dodgers, and San Francisco Giants.

Are You Ready
for the Big Time?

When a young student asked Ike what he liked most about his career as a professional baseball player, Ike said, "Playing in front of thirty to forty thousand people."

-Ike Davis in a 2010 interview with Scholastic News Kids Press

Jason Marquis

Did You Know? The Minnesota Twins were the seventh team Jason played for. However, the Twins were the first American League team.

Jewish Pride

While playing in the minor leagues, Jason never had to deal with the problem of playing on Jewish holidays. According to a *Haaretz* interview, Jason said, "I asked the manager [one Yom Kippur] if I could come to a game as late as possible, and I went to temple to pray. Then I got to the game without eating or drinking. I actually won. The next day I was back in temple."

Biography

Jason Marquis was born on August 28, 1978, in Manhasset, New York, and raised on Staten Island. As a young child, he always had a passion for baseball. At age twelve, Jason led the team South Shore American Little League from

Staten Island, New York. He pitched a no-hitter in the Little League World Series third place game against Canada.

Jason's success on the field continued through high school, where he pitched his school's team to two consecutive New York City championships. While he always had the dream of playing professional baseball, his parents wanted him to go to college. Jason committed to play baseball and attend the University of Miami. In 1996, while Jason was a high school senior, he was drafted in the first round by the World Series champion Atlanta Braves. Jason's parents, especially his mother, who worked for the New York Board of Education, supported his decision to skip college and go straight to professional baseball.

Four years after being drafted, Jason made his first major-league appearance as a relief pitcher for the Atlanta Braves. He is currently playing for his eighth major-league team. In addition to the Atlanta Braves, Jason has played for the St. Louis Cardinals, Chicago Cubs, Colorado Rockies, Washington Nationals, Arizona Diamondbacks, Minnesota Twins, and currently with the San Diego Padres. Jason said, "I feel one of my greatest accomplishments as an athlete is to be able to play in the major leagues as long as I have."

Jason Marquis's Career Highlights

1996 - Iron Horse Award, top player in New York City Public School Athletic League,
Named first-team High School All-American, first-round draft choice of the Atlanta Braves
2005 - Silver Slugger Award, awarded to pitcher with the highest batting average
2006 - World Series champion
2009 - National League All-Star

Mitzvah Moments

Jason said, "All of us have a sense of obligation [to help]. Whether it is time or money, whatever you can do to help, you do. We have a responsibility to give back to the community as Major League Baseball players." Throughout his career, Jason has participated in many charity programs wherever he has played.

Team Player

Jason feels a connection not only to Jewish athletes but all Major League Baseball players. He said, "We all strive for one common goal...to *win*. That is the bond between all Major League Baseball players. I admire all players who work hard and appreciate the game of baseball."

Hometown Hero

When Jason was twelve years old, he pitched a no-hitter against Canada in the Little League World Series third-place game. His parents gave him a replica 15 fifteen-by-fifteen-foot scoreboard of his no-hitter as a Bar Mitzvah gift.

Are You a Believer?

"My advice to a young athlete who aspires to be a profession-al baseball player is to work hard, put in the necessary time to practice all of the skills need-ed to succeed at whatever you want to do. Believe in yourself."

-Jason Marquis

Did You Know? In the off-season, Michael occasionally trains with former world number one tennis star Andy Roddick.

Jewish Pride

"I think it's neat to see other Jewish players. I feel like we are in the golden era for young Jewish baseball players. It is also very cool to interact with Jewish families. We as Jewish people have always loved baseball," said Michael.

Biography

Michael Schwimer was born February 19, 1986, in Fairfax, Virginia. When he was young, he dreamed of playing professional baseball. He played for Central Springfield Little League, and high school baseball and basketball for St. Stephen's & St. Agnes High School in Alexandria, Virginia. While in high school, Schwimer earned four letters in both basketball and baseball. While baseball is what Michael is known for, he was an Independent Schools basketball first-team All-State selection in 2004.

In high school, Schwimer was named the baseball Virginia Independent School League Player of the Year and posted a 9–0 record with 1.04 ERA in 2004. That same year he was named the Alexandria Sportsmen Player of the Year.

Michael continued his career in baseball at the University of Virginia. At the completion of his career there, he had the second most appearances of any pitcher in the history of the school and was fourth in saves. In 2008, Michael was drafted in the fourteenth round of the Major League Baseball draft by the Philadelphia Phillies.

Much of Michael's playing time has been in the minor leagues. He finished the 2011 season with the National League champion Philadelphia Phillies. At the start of the 2012 season, Schwimer played with their Triple-A affiliate, the Lehigh Valley Iron Pigs. In late April of 2012, Michael was once again called up to the Phillies.

Michael Schwimer's Career Highlights

2004 - Named Virginia Independent School Player of the Year in baseball
2005 - February 12, made first collegiate appearance for the University of Virginia
2006 - Set University of Virginia record for appearances, with thirty-six
2008 - Drafted by the Philadelphia Phillies
2011 - August 21, Major League Baseball debut

Mitzvah Moments

Michael has participated in a variety of charity events with teams and individually. He said, "I have been on teams that have hosted games for physically challenged kids. I have been on the field and helped the kids run bases. I hosted and worked an event for autistic children. Additionally, I have given time at camps to teach kids how to play and enjoy the game of baseball."

Team Player

"My junior year of college at the University of Virginia, we were heading to play-offs as a number one seed in the NCAA Regional. Everyone on the team put self aside and came together. We did what we had to do as a team to win," said Michael. Additionally, "Last year (2011) I was with the Phillies the last month of the season. We won the NL East. It was a great experience."

Hometown Hero

Michael's first Major League Baseball appearance came against the Washington Nationals. Nationals Park in Washington, DC, is approximately fifteen minutes away from where Michael grew up in Fairfax, Virginia.

Do You Have the Time?

"My advice to kids is to dedicate your time. The more time you put in, the better you get. Always make sure you are putting in smart time."

-Michael Schwimer

Kevin Youkilis

Did You Know? Like his father, Kevin Youkilis attended the University of Cincinnati, the same university as his childhood hero Sandy Koufax.

Jewish Pride

According to Kevin, "I think all the Jewish ballplayers have a special bond in the pride we all have in our religion and our heritage. We are the minority and take pride in representing our Jewish communities."

Biography

Kevin Youkilis was born March 15, 1979, in Cincinnati, Ohio. After a successful high school career, he played baseball at the University of Cincinnati. While there, Kevin was named an All-American in both 2000 and 2001. Kevin had proven himself as a player with a great eye and the ability to get on base. In 2001, he was drafted in the eighth round of the amateur draft by the Boston Red Sox.

Before being called up to the major leagues, Kevin was named the Red Sox Minor League Player of the Year in 2001 and 2002, and was named to the International League All-Star team in 2003. In addition to his honors during his major-league career, Kevin was the focus of author Michael Lewis's best seller *Moneyball: The Art of Winning an Unfair Game*. The book was the first place Kevin was referred to as "the Greek God of Walks," a nickname that stuck with him and launched him into the national spotlight for the first time. After three years in the minor leagues, Kevin made his Major League Baseball debut on May 15, 2004, against the Toronto Blue Jays. Kevin hit a home run in his second at bat as a major leaguer and helped the Red Sox win 4–0. Kevin played in seventy-two games during his rookie year and walked thirty-three times, living up to his nickname.

While the nickname "Greek God of Walks" is accurate from a batting standpoint, it does not accurately describe Kevin's background. Kevin Youkilis's family is Jewish and originally from Romania. His great-great-great-great-grandfather immigrated to Greece at the age of sixteen to escape the anti-Semitic Cossacks.

Kevin Youkilis's Career Highlights

2000, 2001 - College All-American
2001 - Drafted by the Boston Red Sox
2004 - Major-league debut May 15, 2004
2004, 2007 - World Series champion
2008, 2009, 2011 - American League All-Star

Mitzvah Moments

Off the field, Kevin is dedicated to his charitable foundation, Youk's Kids, which was formed in 2007 as an organization dedicated to the health and well-being of children in need throughout Red Sox Nation. Since its inception, Youk's Kids has raised over $2 million for thousands of kids in need.

"Charity means a lot to me, and I enjoy raising as much money as I can to help out children. As athletes, we have the ability to raise money and bring awareness to causes that we believe in within our communities. I was very blessed to have great parents and a great family that instilled the idea of a mitzvah into my head at a young age."

Team Player

Kevin feels a positive attitude and determination are keys to getting back on the field when injured.

"I love playing baseball and am not a fan of watching from the dugout. For me it's all about listening to the medical staff and not trying to do too much. Doing too much can land you back on the disabled list. [You] have to keep a positive attitude for your teammates and help them out with whatever you can to help win ball games."

Hometown Hero

In 2007 and 2008, Kevin was presented the Jackie Jensen Award by the Baseball Writers' Association of America, Boston Chapter. The award is presented to a Red Sox major-league player for spirit and determination.

Want to become a Big Leaguer?

"My advice to any child that wants to make it professionally is work hard and have fun. Working hard is not just at the sport you play, it's in school too. You can't play sports if you don't get good grades. Having fun is enjoying being around your friends and playing the sport you're participating in. If it becomes too stressful, then it might not be for you. Sports, as a child, are to have fun and compete."

-Kevin Youkilis

May, 2012

Dear Kids,

I retired from sixteen years as a professional baseball player after the 2007 season. I played for the Toronto Blue Jays, the Los Angeles Dodgers, the Arizona Diamondbacks, and the New York Mets. Now, looking back, I realize not only how fortunate I was to have fulfilled my childhood dreams, I also feel a sense of satisfaction for being part of the very exclusive fraternity of Jewish athletes.

In every single stadium throughout North America, young Jewish fans constantly welcomed me. Many of you are now either teenagers or young adults who are pursuing your own dreams. I want to thank all of you from the bottom of my heart. Your support throughout my career added a whole new meaning and purpose to my life as a major leaguer.

Now, as I watch games on TV, I feel a sense of pride for the success that a large number of Jewish major leaguers are having in today's game. Great Jewish players have come before me: Hank Greenberg, Sandy Koufax, and Al Rosen (to name a few), and great Jewish players have come after me: Kevin Youkilis, Ian Kinsler, Ryan Braun, and others. It seems as if the footprint of Jewish baseball stars continues to grow, and I'm honored to be a part of this special group.

Thanks for Your Support,

Shawn Green

Football

Did You Know? Antonio's mother, Marsha, played softball and tennis, and his father Tony, wrestled and played football at Hofstra University.

Jewish Pride

In an online story by the sdjewishjournal.com, Antonio said, "My mom is very proud, knows where she came from, and respects everything about her religion. Every holiday we celebrated, she explained the importance [of them] to us. Even though I am diverse, first and foremost, I am Jewish. It's a big part of me and my family."

Biography

Antonio Garay was born November 30, 1979, in Rahway, New Jersey. Growing up, he was a high school All-American football player as well as a New Jersey state champion wrestler.

After high school, Antonio attended Boston College, where he played football and wrestled. Although his scholarship to Boston College was for football, Antonio became the first All-American in the school's history. While many thought he had Olympic potential, the NFL was where he was headed. During his senior year, Garay was named a captain of the Boston College football team. He graduated with bachelor's degrees in English and marketing, and a master's degree in secondary education with a focus on English. In 2003, Antonio was drafted in the sixth round by the Cleveland Browns. In addition to the Browns, Antonio has played for the Chicago Bears, New York Jets (practice squad), and currently the San Diego Chargers. In 2011 he had a career-high fifty-seven tackles for the Chargers and was named a Pro Bowl alternate.

Garay became a free agent at the end of the 2011–12 season. He was re-signed by the Chargers on March 29, 2012, to a two-year, $6.6 million dollar contract.

Off the field, Antonio is known for his colorful hair and creative hairstyles. Although he is 6′4″ and 320 pounds, Antonio can be seen driving around town in a Hello Kitty Smart Car, one of the smallest cars made.

Antonio Garay's Career Highlights

1998 - New Jersey state wrestling champion and national high school wrestling champion
2000, 2001 - NCAA wrestling All-American
2002 - Voted by teammates as a tri-captain of Boston College football team
2003 - Selected in the sixth round of the NFL draft by the Cleveland Browns
2009 -Inducted in the Boston College Athletic Hall of Fame
2010 - Selected as an alternate to the Pro Bowl

Mitzvah Moments

Antonio has taken part in many charity events to benefit children's causes. He has sold newspapers for the *Union-Tribune* in San Diego to benefit the Rady Children's Hospital. He also is in the process of setting up his charity, Set the Tone Foundation, which will help prepare kids to enter college.

Team Player

In his two years with the Chargers, Antonio has proven to be there for his teammates. He has started in twenty-eight games and played in all thirty-two.

In high school and in college, Antonio was selected as a captain of his team. He captained a New Jersey All-Star team in high school and was elected by his teammates to captain Boston College his senior year.

All in the Family

Antonio comes from the most decorated wrestling family in New Jersey history. His father, brother, and uncles all wrestled. Antonio was the New Jersey state champion and undefeated as a high school senior in the 275 weight class.

Are You Up for the Challenge?

"You're so young you don't know what you can or can't do yet. There are some things that other people can do better than you, but it doesn't mean that you can't do it."

-Antonio Garay, from a 2010 interview with *Insightful Player*

Taylor Mays

Did You Know? Taylor is known for his speed on the football field. Off the field, his speed helped him become a two-time high school Washington state champion in the one and two hundred meters.

Jewish Pride

Speaking of his Bar Mitzvah in a 2006 *Los Angeles Times* interview, Taylor said, "I don't think at the time I really understood what that meant." He added, "Now, looking back on it, I feel like I have come a long way in regard to maturity and becoming an adult. I think that helped me do it."

Biography

Taylor Mays was born February 7, 1988, in Seattle, Washington. His father was a professional football player and was not in favor of Taylor playing football as a child. However, Taylor wanted to follow in his father's footsteps, and although he was a standout in baseball and track, his passion was playing football.

In his junior year at O'Dea High School, Taylor had 89 tackles, 5 interceptions, and 5 deflections. On offense, he caught 25 passes for 614 yards, with 7 touchdowns, and returned 12 punts for 392 yards and 3 touchdowns. He made the Student Sports Junior All-American team. In his senior year of high school, Taylor continued to excel and was named a 2005 *Parade* All-American, *USA Today* All-USA first team, Old Spice Red Zone Player of the Year, Gatorade Washington Player of the Year, All-State first team, and was the All-Metro League Mountain Division Offensive MVP and Defensive Co-MVP pick as a senior defensive back, wide receiver, and quarterback. He had 166 tackles, 5 interceptions, and 5 deflections in 2005, plus caught 36 passes for 765 yards with 15 touchdowns and rushed for 3 more scores.

Taylor committed to playing college football at University of Southern California (USC), where he went on to become a four-year starter and an All-American strong safety.

In the 2010 National Football League draft, Mays was taken in the second round (the forty-ninth overall pick) by the San Francisco 49ers. He played one year in San Francisco and was traded to the Cincinnati Bengals in 2011.

Taylor Mays's Career Highlights

2007 - First-team All-American
2008, 2009 - First- team All-American, first-team All-Pac-10
2010 - Drafted in the second round, forty-ninth overall by the San Francisco 49ers
2011 - August 22, traded to the Cincinnati Bengals
2011 - June 26, Inducted into the Southern California Jewish Sports Hall of Fame

Mitzvah Moments

Taylor participates in many charitable activities, including giving his time to teach kids at football camps. When Taylor was a rookie with the San Francisco 49ers, he helped teach kids at the 49ers' annual youth football camp. According to 49ers.com, "Rookie safety Taylor Mays spoke to the one hundred fifty campers on the importance of respect and listening to your coaches."

Team Player

As a freshman at University of Southern California (USC), Taylor took over the starting safety role after a season-ending injury to a teammate. Taylor played in thirteen games, had sixty-two tackles, team-best three interceptions, and three deflections. He was named to the 2006 *The Sporting News* All-American second team. Taylor went on to start at free safety for the rest of his four-year career at USC.

All in the Family

Taylor's father, Stafford Mays, played professional football as well. Stafford played for the St. Louis Cardinals and the Minnesota Vikings from 1980–1988.

How Will Your Judaism Shape You?

"Some of what makes Taylor Mays a precociously talented safety for USC can be traced back to when he was thirteen. There were months of intense study...Mays was preparing for his Bar Mitzvah. The experience of reading from the Torah shaped him in ways he did not anticipate, ways that have helped him thrive as a person and an athlete."

-According to Gary Klein in a 2006 *Los Angeles Times* story about Taylor Mays

Alex Swieca

Did You Know? Alex did not start playing organized tackle football until after he graduated high school. He had only played flag football and attended football camps.

Jewish Pride

According to Alex, "When my teammates are saying a pregame prayer, I will take the time to say the Shema to myself. I also make sure that I have kosher meals with me when the team travels. A lot of the players on my team have never seen a Jewish football player. I take a lot of pride in teaching them about what I do."

Biography

Alex Swieca was born April 23, 1992, in New York City. Growing up, he always had a passion to play tackle football. However, his desire to play took a backseat to his Judaism. While Alex did play flag football and would practice throwing with his brother, Mike, and his cousin, Michel Cohen (who was a quarterback at the University of Florida), he was unable to play organized tackle football due to his observance of Shabbat. This did not stop him in his drive for competition. While attending Frisch Yeshiva High School in New Jersey, Alex was a member of the wrestling team. He attended the Ken Chertow Wrestling Camps and went on to win two titles at the Yeshiva University national wrestling tournament, known as the Wittenberg Tournament. Although Frisch did not have a tackle football team, Alex continued to play flag football and would work with quarterback coach Tom Martinez (who also coached Tom Brady) in the summers.

Upon graduation from high school in 2010, Alex spent a year in Israel as part of the Young Judaea Year Course program. During this year, his dream of playing tackle football was realized. As a member of the Judean Rebels of the Shabbat-observing Israel Football League, Alex helped lead his team to the Israel Bowl IV title and was named the league's most valuable player.

Alex returned to the United States to attend the University of Michigan. Once again, he kept his dream alive and became a walk-on quarterback at Michigan. Asked why he would rather be at Michigan than going to a smaller college, where he would see more game time, Alex said, "At Michigan there is a tradition of the past. Michigan is about building great people." Although Alex is a walk-on player, he has dressed for Michigan games and played in the most recent Blue-Gold Scrimmage, proving that hard work and determination go a long way in realizing your goals.

Alex Swieca's Career Highlights

2009 and 2010 - Henry Wittenberg Wrestling Tournament Individual Champion 215-pound weight class
2010 - Helped lead Frisch High School to Wittenberg Tournament team title
2011 - Helped lead Israel Football League Judean Rebels to Israel Bowl IV title, named IFL MVP
2011 - Walk-on member of University of Michigan football team as a quarterback, dressed November 19 for first time against Nebraska

Mitzvah Moments

As a college student, Alex stays very busy. However, if you are looking to relax with a Shabbat meal, you can count on him. "I help organize events and meals at Chabad and JRC on the University of Michigan campus," said Alex.

Team Player

When Alex joined the Judean Rebels, he had to win over his team as the new guy. Alex said, "I kept working hard on all those types of things, but when you have so many different types of guys, the only way you can really mesh is to become a family in a way. As the season progressed, so did the maturity of the players and the bond that we built together."

All in the Family

When Alex was growing up, he would play football with his cousin, Michel Cohen, who was a quarterback at the University of Florida, and his brother, Mike, on Saturday afternoons. Years later, as the quarterback for the Judean Rebels, one of his go-to receivers was his brother, Mike.

Making Tough Choices

"Life is all about choices, and there are times when you have to make tough decisions. There are many Jews who are observant of Jewish law who could not continue to advance in their careers. My brother couldn't play in tennis tournaments because they were on Saturdays. When faced with tough choices like Shabbat versus sports, I think it's about making a choice and trying your best, at least that's what I have tried to do. I try to differentiate myself from everyone else by keeping kosher and by observing the holiest holidays, even though it's hard to choose. Just like Sandy Koufax, I would not play on Yom Kippur. Everyone has to make an individual decision. For me, this is a once-in-a-lifetime opportunity [to play at Michigan] and for someone who wants to play sports at a high level, it has to be about how much it means to you."

-Alex Swieca

Did You Know? The Israel Football League plays all of its games on Thursday night, Friday morning, and Saturday night. This allows for those who observe Shabbat to play.

Football Fever in Israel

The Kraft Family Israel Football League is part of American Football in Israel (AFI). There are over a thousand players of tackle and flag football. Tackle football is now being played in the Kraft Family Israel Football League and the Kraft Family High School League. Flag football is being played on men's, women's, and co-ed teams.

In addition to league play, there are Israeli national teams for both men's and women's flag football that compete all over the world. Currently there are plans to form an Israeli national tackle football team.

History of the Kraft Family Israel Football League

The Kraft Family Israel Football League (IFL) is an amateur/semi-pro unpaid football league in Israel. The league played its first season in 2007 with four teams, and plays under the umbrella of American Football in Israel. Tackle football in Israel was being played in parks around the country as pickup games prior to becoming a formal league. The Jerusalem teams and the Judean Rebels play their home games at Kraft Family Stadium in Jerusalem. The stadium is also the site of the Israel Bowl each year. The league and the stadium are named for Robert Kraft and his family. Kraft, the owner of the New England Patriots, has been a financial supporter of the league since its inception.

Today, the league has expanded from four teams to ten teams and two divisions, a North and South Division. The teams in the South Division include the Jerusalem Kings, the Jerusalem Lions, the Judean Rebels, the Be'er Sheva Black Swarm, and the Petah Tikva Troopers. The Northern Division includes the Tel Aviv Sabres, the Tel Aviv Pioneers, the Haifa Underdogs, the Nahariya Northern Stars, and the Herzliya Hammer.

Currently the teams play a ten-game regular season, with play-offs that finish with the Israel Bowl. In the five-year history of the league, there have been four different champions. The Tel Aviv Sabres became the first two-time champion in 2012.

Kraft Family Israel Football League Highlights

2007–2008 - Inaugural season featuring four teams, Jerusalem Lions won Israel Bowl I
2008–2009 - Expanded to five teams, Modi'in Pioneers won Israel Bowl II
2009–2010 - Expanded to seven teams, Tel Aviv Sabres won Israel Bowl III
2010–2011 - Expanded to eight teams and two divisions, Judean Rebels won Israel Bowl IV
2011 –2012 - Expanded to ten teams, Tel Aviv Sabres won Israel Bowl V, first two-time champion

Mitzvah Moments

The Kraft Family Israel Football League definitely does what it can financially as well as in the communities to try to promote charitable activities.

Many of the teams and their players work with youth organizations, on a voluntary basis, to teach them the fundamentals of life and football.

Routinely the league hosts large groups of fans from different social organizations at IFL games for free. The IFL is always looking for more opportunities to show how football truly can be a vehicle of unity within communities.

MVP

In the first five years of the IFL, there have been many players to help their team with great performances during the season and during the Israel Bowl. League Most Valuable Players and Israel Bowl Most Valuable Players include:

2007–2008 League MVP and Israel Bowl I MVP - Moshe Horowitz, Jerusalem Lions 2008–2009 League MVP and Israel Bowl II MVP - Asaf Katz, Modi'in Pioneers 2009–2010 League MVP - Jon Rubin, Jerusalem Kings; Israel Bowl III MVP - Evan Reshef, Tel Aviv Sabres 2010–2011 League MVP - Alex Swieca, Judean Rebels; Israel Bowl IV MVP - Zack Miller, Judean Rebels 2011–2012 League MVP - Chaim Schiff; Israel Bowl V MVP - Adi Hakami, Tel Aviv Sabres

All in the AFI Family

Many of the Kraft Family Israel Football League players began their football career playing in the flag football league. Today, there are players who participate in both leagues at the same time.

Have You Always
Wanted to Play Football?

All of the teams are always looking for new players, both with experience and without. You can e-mail: commissioner@ifl.co.il with any further questions or to be put in touch with your team of your choice.

Mascots

```
S  T  V  A  P  W  I  S  I  M  H  V  S  G  F  L  J  D  H  S  D  W  V  U  Y
Z  M  L  S  K  J  O  R  R  C  R  E  J  V  V  L  A  K  E  Y  Z  X  T  D  B
W  U  T  R  V  U  Z  L  X  H  V  K  A  S  T  T  X  N  L  S  Q  W  T  K  X
S  V  G  E  F  P  M  Z  V  A  U  C  X  L  Y  P  Q  F  E  B  K  L  E  I  K
O  U  N  D  N  G  S  N  R  E  E  S  D  I  U  K  S  E  X  N  R  R  R  D  G
H  Z  F  S  J  G  G  B  T  N  R  N  V  V  T  U  L  V  M  E  O  W  R  N  C
S  F  M  O  S  S  I  X  S  N  O  I  L  E  N  D  T  Y  T  T  P  N  A  O  K
B  T  J  X  E  W  P  L  S  I  H  W  N  D  X  D  T  W  V  S  C  L  P  M  C
F  I  A  L  O  F  N  Y  S  Q  Y  T  E  E  G  L  Y  P  S  A  J  R  I  I  Z
C  A  G  C  Z  U  O  D  M  I  T  V  V  U  S  V  K  A  O  M  I  W  N  Y  T
H  A  E  F  R  Q  R  P  B  R  I  X  N  L  F  I  B  F  L  A  M  E  S  J  X
E  P  V  L  O  A  I  B  O  L  J  Y  O  B  N  R  O  L  C  C  Q  U  I  E  X
W  V  D  R  E  U  E  J  S  U  Y  A  S  R  E  I  L  A  V  A  C  R  R  S  F
S  E  X  I  P  L  A  B  P  J  Z  M  W  S  V  S  G  N  I  K  Y  H  R  T  J
A  W  F  L  N  N  P  S  L  A  T  I  P  A  C  D  C  O  S  Z  K  O  X  A  F
Y  K  I  N  S  Z  S  A  P  W  T  I  G  E  R  S  M  K  G  T  V  W  Q  R  O
Q  K  S  N  I  U  R  B  M  C  H  U  A  K  F  G  B  B  N  A  H  Y  S  S  W
```

1. Shay Doron was one of these in college
2. Omri Casspi was one without a crown in the NBA.
3. Jon Scheyer captained this team to a NCAA title.
4. Jordan Farmar was grizzly while playing for this College
5. Antonio Garay was flying high with this ACC school.
6. Taylor Mays was on his high horse for this team.
7. Alex Swieca throws in the "Big House" for this school.
8. This year's IFL Israel Bowl Champion.
9. Ike Davis was on fire for the Pac-12 team.
10. Michael Schwimer played for this non-kosher AAA team.
11. Jason Marquis was a fearless pitcher for this team.
12. Kevin Youkilis was ferocious for this university.
13. Mike Brown's team wears this symbol of Canada.
14. Mike Cammalleri was not heated about playing for this team.
15. Jeff Halpern returned home to play for this NHL team.
16. Eric Nystrom was one of these for his team.
17. This Israel Football League team won the first Israel Bowl.
18. Omri Casspi and Michael Schwimer both play or played for a team with this name.
19. Jeff Halpern's Ivy League College plays with a roar.
20. Jordan Farmar's current team rhymes with Ike Davis' team.
21. Jason Marquis has only played for one American League team.
22. Kevin Youkilis is not afraid of monsters while playing for this team.

Basketball

Did You Know? Omri is the first Israeli to be selected in the first round of the NBA draft. On October 28, 2009, Omri became the first player from Israel to appear in an NBA game. He scored fifteen points.

Israeli Pride

"Being the first Israeli to play in the NBA, I definitely feel I'm a representative of my country. Whatever I do on and off the court is part of who I am, and I am a proud Israeli. It gives me much motivation to know my country is supporting me," said Omri.

Biography

Omri Casspi was born on June 22, 1988, in Holon, Israel. He began playing basketball in the second grade. Omri worked very hard to improve his play, and by the age of fourteen, he was playing for the junior Maccabi Tel Aviv team as well as the elite high school league in Israel. In addition, Omri was selected to the Israeli under-eighteen team. This gave him experience playing internationally.

Casspi made his professional debut at age seventeen for Maccabi Tel Aviv. He played in Israel for the next three years. Omri caught the attention of many when he played in an exhibition game against the New York Knicks in 2007 at Madison Square Garden. He scored eight points in only sixteen minutes. In 2008, he won the Israeli League Sixth Man of the Year Award and declared himself eligible for the NBA draft.

Omri was selected by the Sacramento Kings with the twenty-third overall pick in the NBA draft. Omri played two seasons with the Sacramento Kings and was traded to the Cleveland Cavaliers in June of 2011.

Omri participates in many Jewish heritage nights around the NBA and often gives his time to speak to young Jewish kids who come out to see him.

Omri is the middle child of Shimon and Ilana Casspi. His older brother, Eitan, was a paratrooper in the Israel Defense Forces and now lives with Omri in Cleveland. His younger sister, Aviv, is currently a member of the Israel Defense Forces.

During the NBA off-season, Omri plays with the Israeli national team.

Omri Casspi's Career Highlights

2009 - Omri drafted in the first round of the NBA draft by the Sacramento Kings
2009 - October 28, Omri made his NBA debut; December 16, Omri made his first NBA start
2010 - January 5, Omri scores a career-high twenty-four points against the Phoenix Suns
2010 - Chosen to play in the NBA All-Star Weekend Rookie Challenge
2011 - June 30, traded to the Cleveland Cavaliers

Mitzvah Moments

In addition to participating in the Juvenile Diabetes Foundation's Viva La Cure gala, Omri donates time, resources, and game tickets to numerous Jewish community groups in cities across the country. He said, "I give my time and money to charity both in Israel and the US, visiting children in hospitals, speaking in events. Wherever I can be of assistance, I try to be. My next goal is to build my foundation in order to raise money and become affiliated with two to three big organizations in Israel and be able to help good causes."

Team Player

When asked about the goals that he sets for himself before every NBA season, Omri said, "I want to keep working hard and keep getting better. I want to be a good teammate and help my team win."

Hometown Hero

Although Omri plays in the NBA, he returns to Israel to play for the Israeli national team in international competition.

Is Your Heart In It?

"I would advise any kid to follow their hearts and dreams. Try to be your best and put your heart into anything you love and would like to do in the future. Hard work and patience pays off and will get you where you want to be. Athletes go through ups and downs. You must stay focused and learn from every experience to get better."

-Omri Casspi

Shay Doron

Did You Know? Shay Doron has been a champion at every level she has played. She has been a high school champion both in Israel and the United States, NCAA champion at the University of Maryland, and EuroLeague champion with Israeli team Elitzur Ramla.

Israeli Pride

Shay has been a member of the Israeli national team and represented Israel in EuroLeague play as a member of Elitzur Ramla. Playing professionally in Israel certainly has been very enjoyable for Shay. "There is something special about looking in the crowd and seeing my friends and family at games," she said.

Biography

Shay Doron was born April 1, 1985, in Ramat Hasharon, Israel. If there is one word to describe Shay, it would be simply "champion." In addition to being a standout basketball player, Shay is also an accomplished track star, winning over sixty medals in a variety of track events in Israel.

After her sophomore year of high school in Israel, Shay moved to New York with her family to play basketball at Christ the King Regional High School in order to pursue her dream of playing professional basketball. Although she was the only Jewish student among the eighteen-hundred-person student body, she had no problems fitting in, especially on the basketball court. In her senior year, Shay led her team to its nineteenth consecutive Brooklyn-Queens title.

Shay was a highly recruited high school basketball player. She decided to play her college career at the University of Maryland. "I wanted to win and build a program that would have continued success. Something clicked between Coach B [Brenda Frese] and me," Shay said. In 2006, she and her fellow Lady Terrapins put it all together to win the NCAA National Championship for the University of Maryland.

Upon graduating from the University of Maryland, Shay was drafted in the second round of the WNBA Draft by the New York Liberty. During the WNBA off-season, she joined Israeli powerhouse Elitzur Ramla and led them to an Israeli league title. Prior to her second year with the New York Liberty, Shay asked for her release from the team. She continued her playing career in Europe, playing in the Romanian league for Municipal MCM Târgovişte, where she won a Romania league cup and a Romania league championship. In 2011, Shay re-joined Elitzur Ramla and led her team to a EuroLeague Championship. In February of 2012, Shay left Israel to sign with UMMC of the Russian League.

Shay Doron's Career Highlights

2003 - First female player from New York named to the McDonald's All-American Team
2004 - Atlantic Coast Conference All-Freshman Team
2006 - University of Maryland National Championship, inducted to the United States Jewish Sports Hall of Fame
2007-Drafted by New York Liberty of the WNBA

Mitzvah Moments

In the off-season, Shay spends her summers teaching girls at her basketball camp in Israel, whose slogan is "Think Outside the Ball." Shay said, "I believe there is so much more to being a great player that has nothing to do with basketball skills. You must have mental toughness and be a good teammate." Doron uses the camp as a vehicle to help foster and develop these qualities in Israeli girls.

Shay is very hands-on and feels it is very important for her to be at the camp everyday to be a teacher and role model to the girls.

Team Player

Shay was a member of the Elitzur Ramla basketball team that won the 2011 EuroLeague Championship. The team also won the Israeli league and the Israeli State Cup. Many consider this team the greatest women's basketball team in the history of Israeli women's basketball.

All in the Family

Shay's parents were both accomplished athletes. Her mother, Tamari, was a member of the Israeli national volleyball team, and her father, Yuda, was a decathlete.

Do You Love the Game?

"My advice to young athletes is to remember that although it [professional sports] seems glamorous, there is a lot of sacrifice involved. You have to decide whether you really love the game. You must really love what you are doing."

-Shay Doron

Jordan Farmar

Did You Know? Jordan Farmar played high school, college, and professional basketball all in the city of Los Angeles.

Jewish Pride

Jordan had the opportunity to play basketball in Israel during the NBA lockout in 2011. He said, "I had the time of my life. The whole country embraced me, and I tried to embrace it. They seemed grateful that I was there, and at the same time, I was so grateful for the opportunity. It was a great change of lifestyle and change of basketball style. It is the best basketball in the world outside of the NBA. For me personally, it was great!"

Biography

Jordan Farmar was born November 30, 1986, in Los Angeles, California. When he was two years old, his parents were divorced, and he went to live with his mother, Melinda. Shortly after her divorce, Jordan's mother remarried Israeli Yehuda Kolani. With a Jewish mother and stepfather, Jordan began celebrating Jewish holidays and Shabbat.

Jordan was a standout basketball player at a young age and played on his high school basketball at Taft High School in Woodland Hills, California. In his senior year, he was named *Los Angeles Times* Player of the Year, as well as California Interscholastic Federation Los Angeles City Section High School Player of the Year, designated Southern California Jewish Athlete of the Year, and earned a *USA Today* Super 25 selection.

After graduation, Jordan attended UCLA and led the Bruins to an NCAA finals appearance in 2006. UCLA lost in the finals to the University of Florida, and Jordan declared himself eligible for the NBA draft. He was drafted in the first round by the Los Angeles Lakers. As a member of the Lakers, Jordan won an NBA Championship in 2009 and 2010. After the 2010 season, Jordan was a free agent and signed a three-year contract with the New Jersey Nets.

In 2011, during the NBA lockout, Jordan signed a contract with Maccabi Tel Aviv, the hometown team of his stepfather, Yehuda.

Jordan Farmar's Career Highlights

2003–2004 - Los Angeles Times High School Player of the Year
2004–2005 – Pac-10 Freshman of the Year, Rivals.com National Freshman of the Year
2006 – First-round NBA draft choice of the Los Angeles Lakers, twenty-sixth pick overall
2009, 2010 - NBA Champion with the Los Angeles Lakers

Mitzvah Moments

Jordan has consistently given back to his community of Los Angeles through the Jordan Farmar Foundation. In addition, he has hosted basketball camps in Israel, raised money for Chabad through a free-throw fundraiser, and hosted a celebrity golf tournament to benefit Mattel Children's Hospital. Jordan said, "I understand how fortunate I am and that I am able to influence kids. A lot of kids admire what I do, and I feel it is important for me to put in time and energy to teach those less fortunate. You never know what you are going to say that sticks with the kids. It is very important to me."

Team Player

Jordan has experienced change during his career. He went from Los Angeles to New Jersey in the NBA and joined Maccabi TelAviv during the NBA lockout.

Jordan said, "The best thing is to approach change with an open mind. A change depends on how you perceive your situation. You should be excited wherever you are. Make the most of where you are. It's all about your attitude."

All in the Family

Jordan Farmar's father, Damon, was a standout football and baseball player. Damon Farmar played Single-A and Double-A baseball for six years.

Is it Worth all the Hard Work?

"My advice to kids is not to by-pass the hard work. A lot of times, kids see the great life an athlete has, but don't get to see the sacrifice put in by the athletes to get to the highest level."

-Jordan Farmar

Did You Know? Jon once scored twenty-one points in seventy-five seconds. Although his team did not win the game, Jon finished the game with fifty-two points.

Jewish Pride

"There are so few Jewish basketball players and athletes playing at a high level. I am proud to be a part of the select group of Jewish athletes that play sports professionally and [are] able to play at an elite university like Duke," said Jon.

Biography

Jon Scheyer was born August 24, 1987, in Northbrook, Illinois. Scheyer was competing on a national level with an AAU team at age nine. By the time he was an eighth grader, he was offered a basketball scholarship to Marquette University in Milwaukee, Wisconsin.

Jon Scheyer attended his local public school, Glenbrook North High School. As a junior, he led his team to the Illinois Class AA State Championship. He is the only player in state history to finish his career ranked in the all-time top ten in points, rebounds, steals, and assists.

In 2006–07 Jon was in the Duke Blue Devils starting lineup as a freshman and led the team in 3-point field goals attempted, free throws attempted, and free throw percentage (.846, third in the Atlantic Coast Conference). He also tied for second on the team with 39 steals.

Prior to his junior year, Scheyer was named one of three captains of the Duke Blue Devils for the 2008–09 season. As a senior, he was once again named captain of the team. Jon became the first Duke player to record 1,400 points, 400 rebounds, 250 assists, 200 3-point field goals, and 150 steals for a career. On April 5, 2010, Jon fulfilled his dream of an NCAA Championship as Duke defeated Butler 61–59.

After graduation from Duke, Jon accepted invitations to NBA team summer camps. While playing for the Miami Heat's summer team in 2010, Jon suffered a life changing eye injury. Since then, he wears protective glasses while playing basketball. Jon has played in the NBA D-League and was a member of Maccabi Tel Aviv in Israel through March of 2012.

Jon Scheyer's Career Highlights

2005 - Member of Glenbrook North High School Illinois State Championship Team
2006 - Named Illinois Mr. Basketball, McDonald's and *Parade* All-American
2007 - Atlantic Coast Conference All-Freshman Team
2009 - Duke University Team Captain, ACC Tournament MVP, All-ACC First Team
2010 - Captain of Duke University National Championship Team, All-ACC First Team

Mitzvah Moments

In 2010, Jon created the Jon Scheyer Foundation. The foundation is dedicated to developing and encouraging the qualities of leadership, dedication, and perseverance in the hearts of young people everywhere, and giving back to underserved communities in need. According to Jon, "It is important to give back to my community, especially the kids. As a kid growing up in Chicago, I always looked up to Michael Jordan and other athletes. I think it is important for the athletes to be a part of the community they are from and the communities they play in."

Team Player

Jon was a member of two championship teams, one in high school and one in college. According to Jon, those teams had a lot in common. "Both teams came together at the right time. We had failures and setbacks, but we were able to come back and overcome. We were able to make runs. In both championship teams, we had played together a lot and we got hot at the right time."

Hometown Hero

Jon's high school basketball team at Glenbrook North High School is the only known high school team to start five Jewish players and win a state championship.

Do Dreams Come True?

"My advice to kids is to have a big imagination and make sure you have big dreams. Make sure you always have fun playing sports. It can get so serious very quickly. Lastly, always listen to your coaches and do what you need to do to get the job done. Make sure you put in the work."

-Jon Scheyer

ACROSS

5. Antonio Garay was a high school state champion in this sport.
9. Jeff Halpern played collegiate hockey at this New Jersey university.
11. Ike Davis plays this position.
13. Jason Marquis pitched a no hitter in the Little League World Series against this country.
14. Mike Cammalleri was drafted by this Los Angeles team.
18. Yuri Foreman is a former WBA champion and future _____.
20. Jordan Farmar played for this university.
22. Shawn Green was drafted by this American League team.
23. Omri Casspi played for this Israeli powerhouse Maccabi.
25. Name of Antonio Garay's Charity.
28. Jeff Halpern would watch this team growing up and eventually played for them.
29. Shahar Pe'er began playing tennis at this age.
31. Ike Davis plays for this National League Team.
34. Dmitry Salita was the subject of this 2007 film.
37. Ike Davis' father played this position.
40. Yossi Benayoun plays professionally for this English Premier League team.
41. Alex Swieca played quarterback for this Israel Football League team.
43. Tamar Katz is a three time Israel National Champion in this sport.
44. Shay Doron was drafted in the WNBA by this New York team.
46. Alex Swieca walked on to this Big Ten football power.
47. Number of NHL teams for which Mike Brown has played.
48. Mike Cammalleri was traded to Calgary from _____.

DOWN

1. Taylor Mays played college football here.
2. Michael Schwimer was born in this state.
3. Yossi Benayoun was born in this southern Israeli city.
4. City where Kevin Youkilis was born.
6. Dmitry Salita won this New York amateur boxing title.
7. Tamar Katz was born in this Texas city.
8. Alex Swieca went to this Jewish High School in New Jersey.
10. Yuri Foreman fought Miguel Cotto in this famous stadium.
12. Taylor Mays was drafted by this NFL team.
15. Jon Scheyer played College Basketball at this ACC Powerhouse.
16. Taylor Mays' father played this sport professionally.
17. Michael Schwimer was drafted by this team.
19. Antonio Garay was drafted by this NFL team.
21. Jordan Farmar won two NBA titles with this team.
24. Eric Nystrom's father Bob played for this NHL team.
26. Morgan Pressel was the youngest winner of a LPGS Major at this age.
27. Round in which Omri Casspi was drafted.
30. Jon Scheyer was the first Jewish American named a _____ All American in high school.
32. Morgan Pressel was born in this Florida city.
33. Jordan Farmar played high school, college and professionally in this city.
35. Eric Nystrom was drafted by this NHL team.
36. Number of Major League teams Jason Marquis has played for.
38. State where Jon Scheyer won a High School State Championship.
39. Omri Casspi was traded to this city from Sacramento.
42. Shahar Pe'er has achieved a career high world ranking of _____.
43. On May 23, 2002 Shawn Green hit ____ home runs in a game.
45. Number of World Series rings Kevin Youkilis has.

Did You Know?

Mike is the proud owner of two cocker spaniels. His dogs are named Max and Benny.

Jewish Pride

Although Mike says that he is not "religious," he did have a Bar Mitzvah. He also had the distinction of playing with another Jewish hockey player in college, Eric Nystrom. The two attended the University of Michigan.

Biography

Mike Brown was born June 24, 1985, in Northbrook, Illinois. Growing up, he played many sports and roller-bladed. Mike's brother brought home a flier about hockey and encouraged their parents to sign up him and Mike to play. Because of his experience roller-blading, Mike was very fast on ice skates. Once he developed the skills needed on the ice, he left all the other sports behind and focused his attention only on hockey.

Mike played youth hockey for the Chicago Young Americans (CYA) of the High Performance Hockey League. In 2000, Brown's CYA team won the national championship. From 2001–2003, he was a member of the United States National Development Team program and played in the North American Hockey League.

For two years, Brown played college hockey at the University of Michigan. In 2004, he was drafted by the Vancouver Canucks in the fifth round, 159 overall. Mike was assigned to the Manitoba Moose, the American Hockey League affiliate for the Canucks.

On December 2, 2007, Mike scored his first goal during his third game in the National Hockey League. Mike ended up playing nineteen games that season.

In addition to Vancouver, Mike has played for the Anaheim Ducks and currently plays for the Toronto Maple Leafs. In 2011, Brown signed a three-year contract extension with Toronto.

Mike Brown's Career Highlights

2000 - Member of the National Champion Chicago Young Americans
2004 - Drafted by the Vancouver Canucks
2007 - December 2, first NHL goal
2009 - Traded to the Anaheim Ducks
2010 - Traded to the Toronto Maple Leafs
2011 - Member of the United States national team

Mitzvah Moments

Mike participates in Athletes T-shirts for Charity. There is a T-shirt called the "Mike Brown Handlebar Destroyer," which has a picture of Mike with his handlebar mustache. All proceeds from the shirts go to the Hospital for Sick Children in Toronto. Mike and the Maple Leafs also have a skills competition for charity. The money raised goes to the NHLPA Goals and Dreams Fund. The Maple Leafs have contributed $2.9 million to the program.

Team Player

Mike was a member of the 2005 US national junior team that competed in the International Ice Hockey Federation World Junior Championship. He also was a member of the 2011 US men's national team.

As one of the toughest forwards in the game, and described as gritty, Mike has always been there to protect his teammates.

Hometown Hero

Growing up near Chicago, Mike had the opportunity to meet some of the Blackhawk players through his parents' business. When he was called up to play his first game for the Vancouver Canucks, Jeremy Roenick called him to wish him luck.

Do You Have Friends Who Play Sports?

"My closest friends at the time were all from hockey, and we played right through junior high school. In high school, a lot of people were playing baseball and football, but I never really got into that. I was more of a soccer and hockey player. As soon as I noticed I was better at hockey than soccer, I just focused on getting better on the ice."

-Mike Brown, March 2012 interview with Kevin Kennedy of *The Hockey News*

Mike Cammalleri

Did You Know? In one of the strangest trades in NHL history, Montreal traded Mike to Calgary during a game in 2012. Mike was pulled from the ice in the second period.

Jewish Pride

According to Mike, "As someone who is from a mixed background, I am very proud of who I am. I celebrate Jewish holidays with my mother's family. My mother's parents are survivors of the Holocaust, and I carry on the pride of who I am. Because of my background, I respect different beliefs that people have."

Biography

Mike Cammalleri was born June 8, 1982, in Richmond Hill, Ontario, Canada. He excelled in many sports growing up, but his love of hockey pushed him to the next level. He played in the Ontario Provincial Junior Hockey League and at age fifteen was named the league's most valuable player. Mike committed to the University of Michigan and at age seventeen graduated high school and began his college career.

During his three years at Michigan, Mike was named to numerous all-star teams and all-American teams. Mike also represented Canada as a member of the Canadian World Junior Championship team during his years in college. In 2001, Cammalleri was drafted by the Los Angeles Kings with the forty-ninth pick in the National Hockey League Amateur Draft.

From 2002–2008, Mike split his time between the Kings and their American Hockey League affiliate, the Manchester Monarchs. In June of 2008, he was traded to the Calgary Flames. In The 2008–2009 season, Mike played in eighty-one games and scored a career-high eighty-two points. In the off-season, Mike signed a multiyear contract with the Montreal Canadiens. On December 28, 2009, he scored the twenty thousandth goal in Canadiens history. In January 2012, Mike was traded to Calgary during a game against the Boston Bruins. He was playing in the game when the deal was finalized, and removed from the ice during the second period. Mike played in sixty-six games between Montreal and Calgary in 2012 and scored forty-one points.

Mike Cammalleri's Career Highlights

1998 - Ontario Provincial Junior "A" Hockey League Rookie of the Year
2001-Central Collegiate Hockey Association First All-Star Team
2002 - NCAA West First All-American Team, drafted forty-ninth overall by the Los Angeles Kings
2002 - November 8, National Hockey League debut with the Los Angeles Kings
2003–2012 - Member Los Angeles Kings, Montreal Canadiens, and currently the Calgary Flames

Mitzvah Moments

According to Mike, "Charity work must be honest and sincere. We have the opportunity to make people happy. As athletes, we can affect in positive ways and [have] positive impacts." Mike has worked with numerous charities, such as Starlight Children's Foundation, World Vision, and SickKids Foundation in Toronto. Additionally, Cammy's Heroes (named for his last name, Cammalleri) donates tickets to Canadian soldiers returning from Afghanistan.

Team Player

During his career, Mike has been an assistant captain for the Canadian world junior team and the Montreal Canadiens. He has also been a team leader in scoring. Mike said, "What makes a team work together is the ability [of teammates] to enable each other to play above their potential."

Hometown Hero

Mike has represented Canada four times, twice as a member of the World Junior Championship team and twice as a member of the World Championship team. In 2007, he was part of the Canadian gold medal team that competed in Moscow.

Do You Have Passion for the Game?

"My advice to kids is to have passion for what you are doing. Enjoy the game, and play as much as possible. Make sure to enjoy the journey. Always challenge yourself in everything you do."

-Mike Cammalleri

Jeff Halpern

Did You Know?

Jeff was the first person from the Washington, DC, area to play for the Washington Capitals.

Jewish Pride

"My role models are Hank Greenberg and Sandy Koufax, not just because they were Jewish but also because they were at the tops of their sports when they were playing. I think Jewish athletes have come a long way since then. I take a lot of pride in that," said Jeff.

Biography

Jeff Halpern was born May 3, 1976, in Potomac, Maryland. When he was a child, his parents, who were Washington Capitals fans, encouraged Jeff to start playing hockey. He was a member of the Little Caps, a team of the best young hockey players in the Washington, DC, area.

Jeff started high school at Churchill High School, his public school in Potomac, which did not have a hockey team. His parents made the decision to send him to St. Paul's School, a prep school in New Hampshire. Although Jeff had a successful high school career, he was not recruited by any Division One colleges. He opted to play a year in Canada. After his year in Canada was finished, Jeff was offered a spot on the Princeton University team.

Jeff played all four years at Princeton and found success on and off the ice. During the 1998 and 1999 seasons, he was selected to the East Coast Athletic Conference (ECAC) all-star team. In 1999, Jeff was selected as the Tigers' captain for his senior season. During his senior year, he scored twenty-two goals and led all players in the ECAC. He was awarded Princeton's Roper Trophy for academic and athletic achievements.

After Jeff left Princeton, he signed with the Washington Capitals as a free agent. He has played a total of seven of his thirteen seasons with Washington, six at the beginning of his career, and in the 2011-2012 season, Jeff rejoined his former team. In between his two stops in Washington, Jeff played for the Dallas Stars, the Tampa Bay Lightning, the Los Angeles Kings, and the Montreal Canadiens.

Jeff Halpern's Career Highlights

1998, 1999 - ECAC second-team all-star
1999 -Awarded Princeton's Roper Trophy for academic and athletic achievement
2000 - Inducted to the Greater Washington Jewish Sports Hall of Fame
2004 - Bronze medalist in Hockey World Championships (Team USA)
2008- Named captain of the United States World Championship team

Mitzvah Moments

Jeff has a special bond to kids and military personnel when it comes to charity work. He said, "I try to visit hospitals and kids and use the celebrity as a hockey player to make those visits enjoyable. I also try to do as much as I can for the military. I tried to meet as many military people as I could in Dallas, Tampa, Washington. I've gotten a lot out of those charities and organizations."

Team Player

Jeff Halpern has proven himself as a leader on the ice at all levels. He was named the Princeton University team captain in 1999, his senior year. As a member of the Washington Capitals, he was chosen team captain for the 2005–2006 season. Once again, the honor of captainship was given to Jeff when he was named team captain of the United States 2008 World Championship team.

All in the Family

Being back in Washington is very special to Jeff. He said, "It's great to be back in a place where I started my career. It is always great to have my father and friends from the area around."

Are We Having Fun Yet?

"Have fun with whatever sport you are playing. You are not going to become a professional when you are five or six years old. Even in high school, the most important thing is to have as much fun as you can. Part of that fun is working hard and improving. If that leads to something greater for the goals you have set, then great. Most important thing is to have fun!"

-Jeff Halpern

Eric Nystrom

Did You Know?

Eric was the 2004–2005 captain of the Michigan Wolverines hockey team in his senior year.

Jewish Pride

According to Eric, "There are not many Jewish professional athletes, so it's definitely special to me. I get a lot of requests to do some really different things because I am Jewish. It's really nice!"

Biography

Eric Nystrom was born on February 14, 1983, in Syosset, New York. He is the son of former New York Islander Bob Nystrom, and excelled in hockey at a young age. In addition to hockey, Eric played many other sports, including baseball and soccer.

Eric represented the United States as a member of the 1999–2000 under-seventeen hockey team, and the 2000–2001 under-eighteen hockey team. Upon graduation from high school, Eric continued his hockey career at the University of Michigan. During his freshman year, he skated for the United States national junior team during the World Junior Championships in the Czech Republic. In June of 2002, prior to his sophomore year of college, Nystrom was selected tenth in the National Hockey League Entry Draft by the Calgary Flames. He played his remaining three years at Michigan before joining the Flames. Eric has great memories of his time at Michigan. He said, "I live and die for Michigan. I am a huge supporter. I would do anything for that school. I follow all the sports teams."

Eric spent his first four years as a professional hockey player splitting time between the NHL and the minor leagues.

In 2009, he played his first full year for the Calgary Flames. He then moved to the Minnesota Wild for the 2010–2011 season and played the 2011–2012 season with the Dallas Stars, where he had his highest point total as a professional.

Eric Nystrom's Career Highlights

2002 – Named to Central Collegiate Hockey Association All-Rookie Team
2002 - First-round NHL draft choice of the Calgary Flames, tenth overall
2005 - October 10, NHL debut against the Colorado Avalanche
2009 - Scored a goal for Calgary in the first round of the Stanley Cup play-offs against Chicago
2010 - Represented the USA at the IIHF World Championship

Mitzvah Moments

As a member of the Calgary Flames, Eric was the player ambassador for the program Reading…Give it a Shot.

He said, "Teachers and parents tell kids to read all the time, but when an athlete says they have a favorite book, kids respond because we play a sport. Knowing this, I feel we have the opportunity to really help out and do something for the kids."

Team Player

Speaking about how special hockey and hockey players are, Nystrom said, "We're more humble because of the origins of the game. Never complain, play through pain, we do everything for the team. We are just regular guys. You can't pick us out of a crowd."

All in the Family

Eric Nystrom and his father, Bob Nystrom, have both been honored by the National Jewish Sports Hall of Fame.

What are Your Goals?

"Becoming a professional athlete takes a lot of sacrifice and hard work. Positive thinking is very important for an athlete. As a young athlete, you must create goals for yourself and stick to them."

-Eric Nystrom

May, 2012

Dear Kids,

As an Israeli national champion, I have had the honor of representing Israel on the international stage for nearly ten years. Every athlete, regardless of what country they are from, feels immense pride and satisfaction in representing their country. Among all the athletes in your division, in your country, it is an honor to know that you were chosen to wear your country's colors and carry its flag on the worldwide stage. This, however, can be said by any athlete, whether they are American, Chinese, Australian, or European. So what makes it so special to be an Israeli Jewish athlete? Why does representing Israel carry even more weight than representing any other country? The answer to that question became apparent to me as a thirteen-year-old in my first international competition representing Israel in Germany. As I took the ice, I heard the announcer say, "Representing Israel," and my name, over the loudspeaker. This was followed by loud shrieks and applause from more than just my three fellow teammates. Since this was not my home country, I was confused as to who was applauding. It turned out that the applause was from local German Jews who came to watch my performance and cheer me on. At the 2010 World Figure Skating Championships in Italy, I was invited by several Italian Jews who attended the event to celebrate Passover Seder with their families. I had the privilege of being welcomed into the hearts of Jews in the Diaspora who were excited to meet an athlete representing Israel. Similar situations happened repeatedly in several countries.

These experiences led me to the realization that not only was I representing Israel, I was representing all Jews. While it was a privilege to represent a nation and a people, and while it was comforting to know that wherever I competed there would always be a strong, supporting, and loving group cheering in the stands, it also made me nervous knowing that so many people were counting on me to represent Israel with respect. Going into competitions, I wanted to medal for myself. However, it became equally as important for me to please the Jewish community that came to support Israel's representative on the international stage. My experience as a young Israeli athlete allowed me to understand the power and love of the Jews in the Diaspora, and the

connection that they feel toward Israel. Having had the privilege of being chosen to compete for Israel has been an extremely rewarding and life-altering
experience.

Sincerely,

Tamar Katz
Olympian, three-time national champion, and four-time world team member

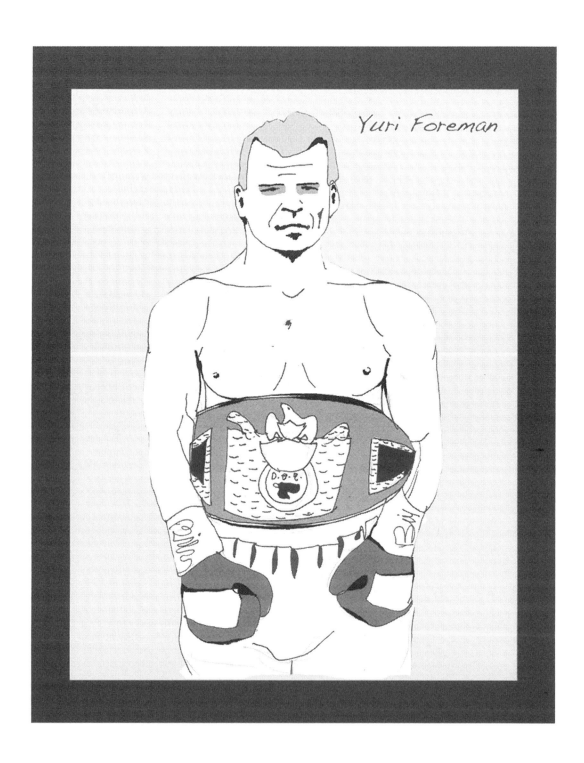

Did You Know? In 2009, Yuri became the first Jewish Israeli to win a world title when he became the WBA super welterweight champion of the world.

Jewish Pride

Yuri is studying to become an Orthodox rabbi and feels that his Judaism is a very important part of his boxing career. He said, "I feel that my Judaism helps me a lot. Boxing is a microcosm of life's challenges. Judaism helps me make a spiritual connection to climb over obstacles."

Biography

Yuri Foreman was born August 5, 1980, in Gomel, Belarus. When Yuri was seven years old, he was beat up by bullies because he was Jewish. His mother decided to enroll him in boxing lessons so that he would be able to defend himself. Yuri and his family immigrated to Israel when he was nine years old. After winning numerous fights and three Israeli boxing titles, he moved to America in 1999 to further his boxing career.

Two years after coming to the United States, Yuri won the New York Golden Gloves tournament. In January of 2002, he officially began his professional career by defeating Felix Israel in a technical knockout. After successfully defeating twenty-seven opponents, Yuri fought Daniel Santos for the World Boxing Association super welterweight title. Yuri won in a twelve-round decision, making him the first Jewish Israeli boxing champion in history. In 2010, Yuri lost his title defense against Miguel Cotto at Yankee Stadium.

Outside of the ring, Yuri is studying to become an Orthodox rabbi. He balances his rabbinic studies with his boxing training. Yuri said, "The ritual of Havdalah is very important to me. Being observant, it helps me make clear separations between being a boxer and going home to be a father and a husband."

Yuri Foreman's Career Highlights

2001 - Became the New York Golden Gloves champion
2007 - North American Boxing Federation light middleweight title win over Saul Roman
2008 - North American Boxing Federation light middleweight title win over James Monroe
2009 - WBA super welterweight title win over Daniel Santos

Mitzvah Moments

Yuri donates 10 percent of all the money he earns from his fights to tzedakah (known as *ma'aser*). Additionally, Yuri is a volunteer for RAJE (Russian American Jewish Experience), where he teaches a class focusing on body and soul. Once a week Yuri teaches a men-only class that combines boxing and Torah skills.

Israeli Pride

Before moving to the United States, Yuri was boxing in Israel as an amateur. During that time, he became a three-time Israeli champion. As a professional boxer, Yuri defended his WBA title in Yankee Stadium against Miguel Cotto. Although he lost the fight in the ninth round by a technical knockout after an injury, Yuri said, "Fighting Cotto in Yankee Stadium was a great experience. I feel very fortunate to achieve something like that. I never thought in my wildest dreams when I came to the United States that I would ever fight in Yankee Stadium. To hear 'Hatikvah' played there was something special."

All in the Family

Yuri is not the only boxer in his family. His wife, Leyla Leidecker, was briefly an amateur boxer and directed the movie about female boxers titled *The Life of Million Dollar Babies*.

You Gotta Believe

"There are no shortcuts in sports. I have seen many athletes come into the gym that are more talented and gifted boxers, but I could beat them by working hard. You can always compensate for what you do not have by working hard. You must have spirituality to be successful as well. Lastly, you must believe in yourself and be confident."

-Yuri Foreman

Shahar Pe'er

Did You Know? At the age of fourteen, Shahar won the Israeli women's championship, making her the youngest player in history to accomplish this.

Israeli Pride

In 2009, Shahar was not allowed to play in the Dubai Tennis Championships because the United Arab Emirates does not have diplomatic relations with Israel and was protesting Israel's actions in Gaza. While this decision was a distraction, it does not change the pride Shahar feels in her home country. Shahar said, "Every time I wear the national uniform, hear the Israeli anthem, and receive so much support from Israelis and Jews around the world it gives me so much pride, power, and motivation."

Biography

Shahar Pe'er was born May 1, 1987, in Jerusalem, Israel. At the age of six, she began taking tennis lessons with her brother and sister. By age twelve, she was playing in competitions and captured the Eddie Herr International Doubles title and finished second in the same tournament in the singles competition. Shahar's success continued on the junior circuit. She became the first Israeli in fourteen years to win a major when, in 2004, she won the Australian Open Junior Championship.

Shahar Pe'er's success on the junior tour had her ranked as high as number two in the world. With her success at the junior level, she made the decision to turn professional late in 2004 and played in International Tennis Federation (ITF) and Women's Tennis Association (WTA) matches. Her first full year, 2005, was filled with accomplishments on and off the court. On the court, Shahar ended with a world ranking of forty-fifth. "This was my first full season of only WTA tournaments. I had to play qualifying rounds in most of the tournaments in the first half of the year. I was happy with the results I had and with the steady progress of my ranking," Shahar said on her website.

Off the court, Shahar did what most Israelis do post high school—she joined the army. She was given the status of "outstanding athlete," which allowed her to continue playing tennis professionally while she served part-time in the army.

In January of 2011, Shahar reached number eleven in the world, the highest world ranking of her career.

Shahar Pe'er's Career Highlights

2001 - Winner of Israeli women's championship at age fourteen
2004 - Winner Australian Open Junior Championship
2006 – Three-time WTA winner in Pattaya Open (Thailand), Prague, and Istanbul
2006–2009 - Voted kids' favorite athlete in Israel
2009 - Winner of tournaments in Guangzhou and Tashkent

Mitzvah Moments

As with many athletes, Shahar Pe'er uses her status as a professional athlete to help those in need. "I donate a lot of my equipment to young Israeli tennis players. I visit a lot of young cancer patients and children with other illnesses," Shahar said of her tzedakah efforts. Additionally, Shahar donates equipment to be auctioned off and plays in charitable tournaments, which helps raise money for children in need. In 2010, Shahar led a March of the Living tour in memory of the victims of the Holocaust for the Jewish Agency for Israel. There were over ten thousand students from around the world, as well as government officials, participating with Shahar.

Team Player

In addition to her accomplishments as a singles player, Shahar has had success as a doubles player as well. She has won three WTA titles and three ITF titles in doubles play. In her six doubles titles, she played with five different players from five different countries. Fellow Israeli Tzipora Obziler was her partner twice.

Hometown Hero

Shahar has represented her country in international play. She played for the Israeli Federation Cup team from 2004–2009 and once again in 2012. Shahar also represented Israel in the 2008 Olympic Games in Beijing.

It's Not All Fun and Games

"Enjoy and like what you do. Otherwise it's not worth it. Work hard. Every professional athlete needs to work hard. It is impossible to get better if you don't. Believe in yourself!"

-Shahar Pe'er

Morgan Pressel

Did You Know? Morgan won the Kraft Nabisco Championship when she was 18 years and 313 days old. She became the youngest woman ever to win an LPGA major championship.

Jewish Pride

Morgan has often said that her Judaism is an important part of her life. In December of 2011, she led a Jewish National Fund mission to Israel. While there, she helped teach young children how to play golf in Caesarea. She said, "I love to see kids pick up a club for the first time. It was a great opportunity for the kids to get out and enjoy the game."

Biography

Morgan Pressel was born on May 23, 1988, in Tampa, Florida. She is the oldest of three children born to Mike Pressel and Kathy Krickstein Pressel. When Morgan was fifteen, her mother died after a four-year battle with breast cancer. After her mother's death, Morgan made the decision to live with her grandparents Evelyn Krickstein and Dr. Herbert Krickstein.

Morgan, like many professional athletes, began playing sports at a very young age. She began playing golf at age eight, and by the time she was twelve years old, Morgan had won four American Junior Golf Association tournaments. Morgan's success on the junior circuit continued, and in 2005, at age seventeen, she made an appeal to be allowed to play professionally. At the time, players had to be eighteen years old to become a member of the Ladies Professional Golf Association (LPGA). In November of 2005, she was granted permission to join the LPGA. In November of 2006, Morgan received her Tour card and toured part-time with the LPGA until her high school graduation in May of 2006.

As a professional, Morgan has won four tournaments, including a major, the Kraft Nabisco Championship. Morgan has been ranked as high as fourth in the world and finished 2011 ranked sixteenth. So far as a professional, Morgan has earned nearly $4.5 million. In addition to playing on the LPGA Tour, Morgan has had the honor of representing the United States in the Solheim Cup in the years 2007, 2009, and 2011. The US won the Solheim Cup in 2007 and 2009.

Morgan Pressel's Career Highlights

2005 - American Junior Golf Association Player of the Year
2006 - American Junior Golf Association Nancy Lopez Award
2007 - Winner of Kraft Nabisco Championship
2008 - Winner of Kapalua LPGA Classic
2010 - LPGA of Japan Tour, winner of World Ladies Championship Salonpas Cup

Mitzvah Moments

The Morgan Pressel Foundation has raised over $2 million for the Lynn Cancer Institute's Breast Cancer Center at Boca Raton Community Hospital, Sylvester Cancer Center at the University of Miami, and Hospice by the Sea. Morgan said, "The foundation means everything to me. It's like my baby. I am very proud of it, and it is very important to me. I work on the foundation year-round and am always trying to raise money and awareness. Golf has given me the platform to be able to hold golf tournaments to raise money and change lives in Florida."

Team Player

Morgan has represented the United States in the Solheim Cup (a competition between European and American women's golfers) once as an amateur and three times as a professional. In 2007 and 2009, Morgan was part of the team of Americans that won the cup. Her career record in Solheim Cup competition is seven wins, two losses, and two halves. "One of the proudest moments I have had in golf was winning the Solheim Cup for the United States in 2009," said Morgan.

All in the Family

Morgan is not the first professional athlete in her family and may not be the last. Her uncle, Aaron Krickstein, was a WTA top-ten professional tennis player, and her sister Madison is a member of the University of Texas women's golf team.

It's Not as Easy as it Looks!

"Have fun, and make sure you enjoy what you are doing. Being a professional athlete is not easy. It is a grind even though it looks great on television. It is all about input-output. The more you work you put in, the more you will get out."

-Morgan Pressel

Yossi Benayoun

Did You Know? When

Yossi was eighteen, he joined the Israel Defense Forces, as most eighteen-year-olds do. He served as a sports instructor in the navy for three years. Yossi's status as an elite athlete allowed him to play soccer during his army service.

Israeli Pride

Yossi Benayoun has represented Israel in international play since 1998. In 2006, he was named Israeli national team captain. He said, "This is the biggest event, a tremendous achievement in my career." On September 2, 2010, Yossi scored a hat trick (three goals) against Malta in a 3–1 win.

Biography

Yossi Benayoun was born May 5, 1980, in Dimona, Israel. Yossi's talent and soccer skill were recognized at an early age. At nine years old, he began playing for the Hapoel Be'er Sheva youth team. By the age of fifteen, his play received notice from European Soccer club Ajax in the Netherlands. He moved to Amsterdam with his family, and his play earned him his first professional contract with the team. Yossi made the decision to turn the contract down and move back to Israel. He missed Israel and his girlfriend Mirit, who is now his wife.

After his return to Israel, Yossi began his professional career at age sixteen with Hapoel Be'er Sheva. Within Israel, he also played for Maccabi Haifa. In 2002, Yossi joined his first professional team in Europe when he left Israel to play for Racing de Santander, which plays in Spain's La Liga. After leaving Spain, Yossi went to play in the English Premier League. He played for West Ham United, Liverpool, and Chelsea. Currently, Yossi is on loan from Chelsea and plays for Arsenal.

In addition to league play, Yossi has been a member of the Israeli national team, where he has been the team captain since 2006.

Yossi has been given two different nicknames during his career. He has been called "The Kid" and "The Diamond from Dimona."

Yossi Benayoun currently lives with his wife and kids in London, England.

Yossi Benayoun's Career Highlights

1995–1996 – Highest scorer AJAX youth team (Netherlands) highest scorer, offered four-year professional contract to play for their professional team
1998–Present - Member of the Israeli national team
2001 - Israeli Footballer of the Year
2002-2012-Member of Racing de Santander, West Ham United, Liverpool, Chelsea, Arsenal

Mitzvah Moments

Yossi gives back to his community in a variety of ways. In the past, he has worked with One Family, an organization focused on changing lives of those who are victims of terror or war. Yossi, One Family, and Arsenal hosted eighteen Israelis in London. They shared a Shabbat meal and attended an Arsenal game and met all of the team's players. Yossi was so impressed with the group that after his game, he met them at the airport before they departed England to go back to Israel. The purpose of the trip was to give the visitors a welcome break from their ongoing medical treatments.

Team Player

In professional sports, players move around to other teams often. When Yossi arrived to play for Chelsea, he said, "There are a lot of good players, big players. For me it is the beginning, and I have to work hard and prove I can bring something to this club. The only thing I can promise is I will work hard and do my best, and hopefully it will be good enough."

All in the Family

When Yossi was young, his father could not afford to put him on a bus to Be'er Sheva, where he was training with Hapoel Be'er Sheva. His father would hitchhike with him sixty kilometers (thirty-six miles) to get to practice.

Are You Ready to
Lead Your Team?

"It was a lot of pressure, but I call it positive pressure. It was the pressure that every player wants. Since I started, I wanted to be the best, to be the best on the national team, to be one of the leaders."

-Yossi Benayoun in a 2005 interview with LFCHistory.net, speaking about joining Maccabi Haifa

Dear Kids:

My name is Dmitriy Salita and I am a professional boxer. I was born in Odessa, Ukraine. My family and I immigrated to New York City when I was 9 years old. Until I was 9, I did not know much about what it meant to be a Jew. Growing up in New York city
seeing religious Jewish people I started to educate myself about
our wonderful history.
I joined a boxing gym when I was 13 years old. I won the US Championships and the Golden Gloves and after that decided to turned professional, I was 19 years old.
As the first and only religious boxer in the world, I felt different but in a good way. I knew that I had an opportunity to represent my people through my sport, not only in the ring but also outside it. I always felt connected to G-D and felt that he was guiding me and helping
me through good times and rough times. A Rabbi once told me that G-D loves hard focused work.

In life we have ups and downs, challenges and triumphs. We all have unique talents, special skills and are where we are for a reason. That reason is to make the world a better place, to be nice, kind, strong ,courageous
and to represent ourselves proudly amongst our Jewish friends. But even more importantly in our contact with the rest of the world. My hardest times in the ring helped me become closer to G-D. I felt that it was always very important to connect to G-D especially as he relates to you.

The greatest thing that I have done in my career was stay committed to my faith and represented my people. You have special talents and have the ability to illuminate your place in the world, light it up.

Dmitriy Salita

ANDREW GERSHMAN

Mascots

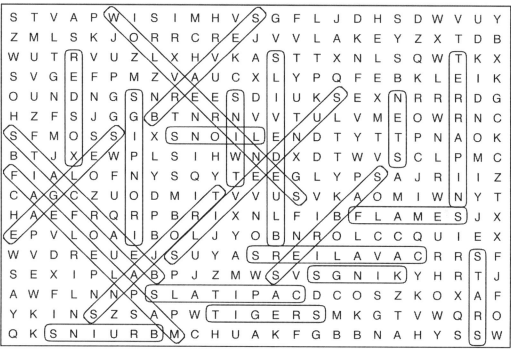

1. Shay Doron was one of these in college [TERRAPIN]
2. Omri Casspi was one without a crown in the NBA. [KINGS]
3. Jon Scheyer captained this team to a NCAA title. [BLUEDEVILS]
4. Jordan Farmar was grizzly while playing for this College [BRUINS]
5. Antonio Garay was flying high with this ACC school.   [EAGLES]
6. Taylor Mays was on his high horse for this team. [TROJANS]
7. Alex Swieca throws in the "Big House" for this school. [WOLVERINES]
8. This year's IFL Israel Bowl Champion. [SABRES]
9. Ike Davis was on fire for the Pac-12 team. [SUNDEVILS]
10. Michael Schwimer played for this non-kosher AAA team. [IRONPIGS]
11. Jason Marquis was a fearless pitcher for this team. [BRAVES]
12. Kevin Youkilis was ferocious for this university.   [BEARCATS]
13. Mike Brown's team wears this symbol of Canada. [MAPLELEAF]
14. Mike Cammalleri was not heated about playing for this team. [FLAMES]
15. Jeff Halpern returned home to play for this NHL team. [CAPITALS]
16. Eric Nystrom was one of these for his team. [STARS]
17. This Israel Football League team won the first Israel Bowl. [LIONS]
18. Omri Casspi and Michael Schwimer both play or played for a team with this name. [CAVALIERS]
19. Jeff Halpern's Ivy League College plays with a roar. [TIGERS]
20. Jordan Farmar's current team rhymes with Ike Davis' team. [NETS]
21. Jason Marquis has only played for one American League team. [TWINS]
22. Kevin Youkilis is not afraid of monsters while playing for this team. [REDSOX]

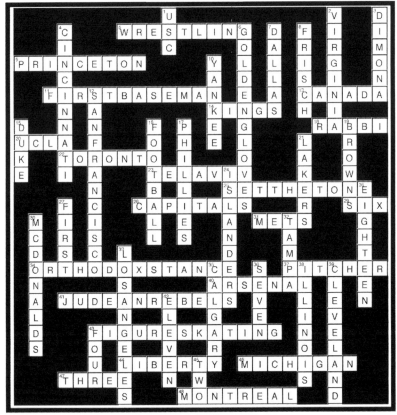

ACROSS

5. Antonio Garay was a high school state champion in this sport.
9. Jeff Halpern played collegiate hockey at this New Jersey university.
11. Ike Davis plays this position.
13. Jason Marquis pitched a no hitter in the Little League World Series against this country.
14. Mike Cammalleri was drafted by this Los Angeles team.
18. Yuri Foreman is a former WBA champion and future _____.
20. Jordan Farmar played for this university.
22. Shawn Green was drafted by this American League team.
23. Omri Casspi played for this Israeli powerhouse Maccabi.
25. Name of Antonio Garay's Charity.
28. Jeff Halpern would watch this team growing up and eventually played for them.
29. Shahar Pe'er began playing tennis at this age.
31. Ike Davis plays for this National League Team.
34. Dmitry Salita was the subject of this 2007 film.
37. Ike Davis' father played this position.
40. Yossi Benayoun plays professionally for this English Premier League team.
41. Alex Swieca played quarterback for this Israel Football League team.
43. Tamar Katz is a three time Israel National Champion in this sport.
44. Shay Doron was drafted in the WNBA by this New York team.
46. Alex Swieca walked on to this Big Ten football power.
47. Number of NHL teams for which Mike Brown has played.
48. Mike Cammalleri was traded to Calgary from _____.

DOWN

1. Taylor Mays played college football here.
2. Michael Schwimer was born in this state.
3. Yossi Benayoun was born in this southern Israeli city.
4. City where Kevin Youkilis was born.
6. Dmitry Salita won this New York amateur boxing title.
7. Tamar Katz was born in this Texas city.
8. Alex Swieca went to this Jewish High School in New Jersey.
10. Yuri Foreman fought Miguel Cotto in this famous stadium.
12. Taylor Mays was drafted by this NFL team.
15. Jon Scheyer played College Basketball at this ACC Powerhouse.
16. Taylor Mays' father played this sport professionally.
17. Michael Schwimer was drafted by this team.
19. Antonio Garay was drafted by this NFL team.
21. Jordan Farmar won two NBA titles with this team.
24. Eric Nystrom's father Bob played for this NHL team.
26. Morgan Pressel was the youngest winner of a LPGS Major at this age.
27. Round in which Omri Casspi was drafted.
30. Jon Scheyer was the first Jewish American named a _____ All American in high school.
32. Morgan Pressel was born in this Florida city.
33. Jordan Farmar played high school, college and professionally in this city.
35. Eric Nystrom was drafted by this NHL team.
36. Number of Major League teams Jason Marquis has played for.
38. State where Jon Scheyer won a High School State Championship.
39. Omri Casspi was traded to this city from Sacramento.
42. Shahar Pe'er has achieved a career high world ranking of _____.
43. On May 23, 2002 Shawn Green hit _____ home runs in a game.
45. Number of World Series rings Kevin Youkilis has.

Sources

Ike Davis

"*Ike Davis (davisik02).*" BaseballReference.com. 5 Apr 2012. http://www.base-ball-reference.com/bullpen/Ike%20Davis%20(davisik02) (accessed Apr 17).

Shark, Shannon. "*The Mets Police.*" 26 Jun 2011. http://metspolice.com/2011/06/26/ike-davis-charity-dinner/ (accessed Mar 12, 2012).

Obert, Richard. "*Friends, family remember ex-Chaparral baseball player Michael Lio with fundraiser Read more:* http://www.azcentral.com/sports/preps/ne/articles/2010/07/23/20100723michael-lio-chaparral-fundraiser.html (accessed Feb 13, 2012).

"*Ron Davis.*" Baseballreference.com. http://www.baseball-reference.com/players/d/davisro02.shtml (accessed Feb 13, 2012).

"*Ike Davis.*" Jewish Baseball News. http://www.jewishbaseballnews.com/players/ike-davis/ (accessed Feb 13, 2012).

"*Ike Davis.*" New York Mets. http://newyork.mets.mlb.com/team/player.jsp?player_id=477195#gameType=%27S%27 (accessed Feb 13, 2012).

O'Conner, Joseph. "*Meet Met's Ike Davis.*" Scholastic News. 6 Jun 2010. http://blogs.scholastic.com/kidspress/2010/07/meet-mets-ike-davis.html (accessed Feb 13, 2012).

Jason Marquis

Orgad, Yaniv. "*MLB's Jewish pitcher balances fastballs, faith and family.*" Haaretz. 17 Aug 2009. http://www.haaretz.com/print-edition/sports/mlb-s-jewish-pitcher-balances-fastballs-faith-and-family-1.282143 (accessed Feb 20, 2012).

"*From the Little League World Series to the Major Leagues, Jason Marquis is Always Looking to Make His Best Pitch.*" Little League Baseball Online. 2 Oct 2009. http://www.littleleague.org/media/newsarchive/2009/sep-dec/jason-marquisllws.htm (accessed Feb 20, 2012).

"*Jason Marquis.*" *Baseballreference.com.* *http://www.baseball-reference. com/players/m/marquja01.shtml (accessed Feb 19, 2012).*

Michael Schwimer

Callahan, William. "*Springfield's Own Michael Schwimer to Pitch for Philadelphia Phillies .*" Kingstowne-RosehillPatch. 17 Aug 2011. http://kings-towne.patch.com/articles/springfields-own-michael-schwimer-to-pitch-for-philadelphia-phillies (accessed Feb 27, 2012).

"*Michael Schwimer Biography.*" University of Virginia. 19 Jul 2007. http://www.virginiasports.com/ViewArticle.dbml?DB_OEM_ID=17800&ATCLID=1134169 (accessed Feb 27, 2012).

"*Michael Schwimer.*" baseballreference.com. http://www.baseball-reference. com/players/s/schwimi01.shtml (accessed Feb 27, 2012).

Kevin Youkilis

"*About Us-Kevin Youkilis.*" Kevin Youkilis-Hits for Kids. http://www.youkskids. org/Kevin-Youkilis-Charity.html (accessed Mar 5, 2012).

"*Kevin Youkilis.*" baseballreference.com. http://www.baseball-reference.com/ players/y/youklke01.shtml (accessed Mar 5, 2012).

Fenwayfanatics.com. http://www.fenwayfanatics.com/redsox/player/kevin_youkilis/ (accessed Mar 5, 2012).

Gleeman, Aaron. "*Kevin Youkilis placed on 60-day DL, done for season.*" NBC Sports. 28 Sep 2011. http://hardballtalk.nbcsports.com/2011/09/28/playoffs-or-not-kevin-youkilis-unlikely-to-play-again-this-year/ (accessed Mar 5, 2012).

Antonio Garay

"*Players-Antonio Garay.*" San Diego Chargers. 12 2012. http://www.chargers.com/team/roster/Antonio-Garay/a1a92150-240b-4c64-9233-dd671f116723 (accessed Mar 12, 2012).

Seymour, Joey. "*Jewish Charger Antonio Garay strives to help bring San Diego a Super Bowl championship.*" SdJewishWorld. 13 Jan 2010. http://sdjewish-world.wordpress.com/2010/01/13/jewish-charger-antonio-garay-strives-to-help-bring-san-diego-a-super-bowl-championship/ (accessed Mar 12, 2012).

"*Antonio Garay-Set The Tone.*" Antonio Garay. http://setthetone.net/ (accessed Mar 12, 2012).

Taylor Mays

Klein, Gary. "*Coming of Age.*" Los Angeles Times . 29 Dec 2006. http://articles.latimes.com/2006/dec/29/sports/sp-mays29 (accessed Mar 19, 2012).

"*Taylor Mays.*" Jewish Virtual Library. 2012. http://www.jewishvirtuallibrary.org/jsource/biography/taylormays.html (accessed Mar 19, 2012).

"*Player Bio: Taylor Mays.*" USCtrojans.com. http://www.usctrojans.com/sports/m-footbl/mtt/mays_taylor00.html (accessed Mar 19, 2012).

Price, Taylor. "*Youth Camp: Rookies Rathman and More.*" 49ers.com. 13 Jul 2010. http://blog.49ers.com/2010/07/13/youth-camp-rookies-rathman-and-more/#mo re-2578 (accessed Mar 19, 2012).

Israel Football League

"*IFL-Kraft Family Israel Football League.*" Israel Football League. http://www. ifl.co.il/ (accessed Mar 26, 2012).

Omri Casspi

"*Omri Casspi.*" NBA.com. http://www.nba.com/playerfile/omri_casspi/bio. html (accessed Apr 2, 2012).

Reed, Tom. "*Cavaliers' Omri Casspi embraces inspirational role he serves.*" Cleveland.com. 23 Apr 2012. Cavaliers' Omri Casspi embraces inspirational role he serves (accessed Apr 2, 2012).

"*OmriCasspi.com homepage.*" Omri Casspi. http://www.casspi18.com/index. php/site/language/1.html (accessed Apr 2, 2012).

Shay Doron

"*Shaydoron.com official website.*" Shay Doron. 2007. http://www.shaydoron. net/ (accessed Apr 3, 2012).

"*Shay Doron-Player Bio.*" *University of Maryland. http://www.umterps.com/ sports/w-baskbl/mtt/doron_shay00.html (accessed Apr 3, 2012).*

Jerusalem Post. http://fr.jpost.com/servlet/Satellite?pagename=JPost/ JPArticle/ShowFull&cid=1129540635307 (accessed Apr 3, 2012).

"*Shay Doron.*" Jewish Virtual Library. http://www.jewishvirtuallibrary.org/ jsource/biography/Shay_Doron.html (accessed Apr 3, 2012).

Jordan Farmar

"*Jordan Farmar.*" Jewish Virtual Library. http://www.jewishvirtuallibrary.org/ jsource/biography/Jordan_Farmar.html (accessed Jan 23, 2012).

"*Jordan Farmar Foundation.*" JordanFarmar. 2010. *http://www.farmargives. org/ (accessed Jan 23).*

Jon Scheyer

"*JonScheyer homepage.com.*" Jon Scheyer. http://jonscheyer.com/ (accessed Feb 6, 2012).

"*SI Vault Jon Scheyer.*" Sports Illustrated. http://sportsillustrated.cnn.com/ vault/article/web/COM1047782/index.htm (accessed Feb 6, 2012).

"*Honoree Details-Jon Scheyer.*" Jewish Sports Hall of Fame. http://www.jewishsports.org/jewishsports/detail.asp?sp=272 (accessed Feb 6, 2012).

Mike Brown

"*Players-Mike Brown.*" National Hockey League. http://www.nhl.com/ice/ player.htm?id=8471371&view=news (accessed Feb 13, 2012).

"*Mike Brown Profile.*" SB Nation. http://www.sbnation.com/nhl/players/54463/mike-brown# (accessed Feb 12, 2012).

Kennedy, Kevin. "*Mike Brown.*" The Hockey News. 3 Mar 2012. http://www. thehockeynews.com/articles/45222-Mike-Brown.html (accessed Feb 12, 2012).

"*Athletes T-Shirts for Charity.*" Sports Chirps. 2011. (accessed Feb 14, 2012).

Hudes, Sammy. " *Jewish NHLers Pass the Torch.*" Shalom Life. 8 Jul 2010. http:// www.shalomlife.com/news/13234/jewish-nhlers-pass-the-torch/ (accessed Feb 14, 2012).

Weber, M. "Q & A ... with Canucks tough guy Mike Brown." Canada.com. 30 Nov 2008. http://www.canada.com/theprovince/news/story.html?id=c87977db-915a-4d0a-8424-01f3c08e3ac1 (accessed Feb 21, 2012).

"Team Blue Defeats Team White In Skills Competition." Toronto Maple Leafs. 14 Nov 2010. http://mapleleafs.nhl.com/club/news.htm?id=543484.

Chicago Young Americans. http://www.cyahockey.com.prod.ngin.com/ page/show/96911-boys-alumni (accessed Feb 16, 2012).

Smith, Mike. "Mike Brown of the Toronto Maple Leafs." Fighting for Stanley. 27 Mar 2012. http://www.fightingforstanley.ca/toronto/mike-brown-of-the-toronto-maple-leafs/ (accessed Apr 5, 2012).

USA Hockey Magazine. http://www.usahockey.com/Template_Usahockey. aspx?NAV=TU_01_03&id=303880 (accessed Feb 10, 2012).

Mike Cammalleri

"*Mike Cammalleri.*" National Hockey League. http://www.legendsofhockey. net/LegendsOfHockey/jsp/SearchPlayer.jsp?player=20170 (accessed May 13, 2012).

Mccollough, J. B.. "Mike Cammalleri has always been The Wolverines'' Mr. Everything discusses the upcoming season and what it will take for Michigan ." The Michigan Daily. 3 Oct 2001. http://www.michigandaily.com/content/ mike-cammalleri-has-always-beenthe-wolverines-mr-everything-discusses-upcoming-season-and-wh (accessed Feb 10, 2012).

"*Mike Cammalleri.*" Jewish Virtual Library. http://www.jewishvirtuallibrary. org/jsource/biography/Cammalleri.html (accessed Mar 13, 2012).

Duquette, Jr, Dan. "Michael Cammalleri Traded to Calgary Flames Mid-Game After Canadiens Pull Winger Off Ice Against Bruins Read more at: http://www. nesn.com/2012/01/report-michael-cammalleri-traded-to-calgary-flames-mid-game-after-canadiens-pull-winger-off-ice-agai.html." New England Sports Network. 13 Jan 2012. http://www.nesn.com/2012/01/report-michael-cam-malleri-traded-to-calgary-flames-mid-game-after-canadiens-pull-winger-off-ice-agai.html (accessed Mar 12, 2012).

AP. *"Cammalleri scores Habs' 20,000th goal."* ESPN. 28 Dec 2009. http://sports. espn.go.com/nhl/news/story?id=4777534 (accessed Feb 10, 2012).

Eric Nystrom

"Eric Nystrom-Dallas Stars." National Hockey League. http://stars.nhl.com/ club/player.htm?id=8470180 (accessed Mar 19, 2012).

"Honoree Details- Eric Nystrom." Jewish Sports Hall of Fame. http://www.jew-ishsports.org/jewishsports/detail.asp?sp=130 (accessed Feb 20, 2012

Hudes, Sammy. *"Interviews with 'Top Jews In Sports'- Eric Nystrom."* Shalom Life. 6 Sep 2011. http://www.shalomlife.com/culture/15880/interviews-with-top-jews-in-sports-eric-nystrom/ (accessed Feb 21, 2012).

Jeff Halpern

"Jeff Halpern." Jewish Virtual Library. http://www.jewishvirtuallibrary.org/ jsource/biography/Jeff_Halpern.html (accessed Feb 27, 2012).

El-Bashir, Tarik. *"Capitals' Halpern Acts on Faith."* The Washington Post. 12 Oct 2005. http://www.washingtonpost.com/wp-dyn/content/article/2005/10/11/ AR2005101101664.html (accessed Feb 27, 2012).

Yossi Benayoun

"Yossi Benayoun: The Kid from Dimona." LFCHistory.net. 2005. http://www. lfchistory.net/Articles/Article/2036 (accessed Feb 28, 2012).

Wilson, Jeremy. *"Arsenal striker Robin van Persie outshone by Yossi Benayoun on night of landmark goals."* The Telegraph. 22 Dec 2011. http://www.tele-graph.co.uk/sport/football/competitions/premier-league/8971321/Arsenal-striker-Robin-van-Persie-outshone-by-Yossi-Benayoun-on-night-of-landmark-goals.html (accessed Feb 28, 2012).

"*Yossi Benayoun-Stats.*" ESPN. http://soccernet.espn.go.com/player/_/ id/19091/yossi-benayoun?cc=5901 (accessed Mar 1, 2012).

"*Yossi Benayoun Greets One Family Injured Soldier Group.*" One Family. 2010. http://www.onefamilyuk.org/one-family-group-arrives-in-london/ (accessed Mar 1, 2012).

"*Yossi Benayoun .*" chelseaafc.com. http://www.chelsefc.com/page/ OnLoanPlayersDetails/0,,10268~2083913,00.html (accessed Mar 1, 2012).

Yuri Foreman

Lole, Kevin. "*Rooting for Yuri Foreman is cheering on greatness.*" Yahoo Sports. 10 Mar 2011. http://sports.yahoo.com/box/news?slug=ki-yuriforeman031011 (accessed Jan 10, 2012).

Last, Jeremy. "*Boxing: Israel's own Foreman gets his shot at a belt.*" Jerusalem Post. 13 Nov 2009. http://www.jpost.com/Sports/Article.aspx?id=160321 (accessed Jan 17, 2012).

Buchanan, Jason. "*The Life of Million Dollar Babies.*" Fandango. http://www. fandango.com/thelifeofmilliondollarbabies_v430517/plotsummary (accessed Jan 30, 2012).

"*Yuri Foreman Homepage.*" Yuri Foreman. http://www.yuriforeman.com/ (accessed Jan 30, 2012).

Shahar Pe'er

"*Shahar Pe'er Official Website.*" Shahar Pe'er. http://www.shaharpeer.co.il/ (accessed Mar 14, 2012).

"*WTA Players Shahar Pe'er.*" WTA. http://www.wtatennis.com/player/shahar-peer_2257889_10493 (accessed Mar 21, 2012).

Canadian Press. "*Israel's Shahar Peer serves in the military*." Women's Tennis Blog. 20 Sep 2007. http://www.womenstennisblog.com/2007/09/20/israels-shahar-peer-serves-in-the-military/ (accessed Mar 21, 2012).

Morgan Pressel

"*Morgan Pressel-Golf Professional.*" Morgan Pressel. http://www.morgan-pressel.org/ (accessed Jan 2, 2012).

"*Morgan Pressel.*" LPGA. http://www.lpga.com/golf/players/p/morgan-pressel.aspx (accessed Jan 2, 2012).

"*Morgan Pressel Foundation.*" Morgan Pressel. http://www.morganpressel-foundation.com (accessed Apr 18, 2012).

Gross-Rhode, Dana. "*Q&A with Morgan Pressel.*" Golf 365. 11 Apr 2007. http://www.golf365.com/features_story/0,17923,9787_2051888,00.html (accessed Mar 13, 2012).

Made in the USA
Charleston, SC
26 November 2012